To Brian from his loving wife, Frances

7. Jan 1991

LONDON BUSES
1929 ~ 1939

LONDON BUSES 1929~1939

Gavin Martin

LONDON TRANSPORT MUSEUM

LONDON
IAN ALLAN LTD

Contents

First published 1990

ISBN 0 7110 1880 4

Published by Ian Allan Ltd, Shepperton, Surrey; and printed by Ian Allan Printing Ltd at their works at Coombelands in Runnymede, England

The author wishes it to be understood by readers that the insertion of hyphens in the text in most cases represents the choice and style of the publisher and not those of the author, as also does the layout of some of the illustrations.

Author's Preface

Although this book is essentially about the buses I knew in my boyhood in the 1930s, the fact that I have enough to say about them to fill a book is a result of three accidents of history. The first of these was the revolution in bus design which took place in 1929 with the appearance of the new range of AEC chassis designed by John Rackham and their adoption by the London General Omnibus Co. The second was the formation of the London Passenger Transport Board in July 1933, which six years later had resulted in the replacement of all the buses it had inherited except for AEC models of Rackham's design. The third was the outbreak of war in September 1939, which had the effect of prolonging the life of all the types then in service for another 10 years or more. I was only 12 when the war began, but by the time it ended I was 18 and correspondingly better able to understand the significance of the things which were still there to be seen and heard. Whilst I have filled in by research the gaps left by buses and coaches belonging to those types of which I did not have personal knowledge, I must leave it to others to do justice to the vehicles which had disappeared from the London scene before the war began.

As regards my sources, a fruitful one to which I gained access in 1945 was the University Library at Cambridge, where all back numbers of trade journals are kept just as they came out with their original advertising. A still better opportunity came in 1946 when I was accepted for a vacation course at Chiswick Works and through the kindness of the late Mr E. C. Ottaway, the Works Manager, I was allowed access to the records kept in the Rolling Stock Office. About this time I had the good fortune to meet Dr Andrew Gilks who shared the same interests and this book includes much material which originally came from him. It also owes a great deal to Alan Townsin, to whose kindly help and advice I have had access for almost as long. There have also been many others who would not wish to be mentioned whose help in various ways I acknowledge with gratitude.

A particularly enjoyable part of the experience has been choosing the illustrations. One of London Transport's less widely known activities was to maintain an archive of photographs, now in the care of the London Transport Museum. This includes a splendid collection of street scenes going back to horse bus days, some appealing examples of which are included among the 40-odd photographs from this source which will be found in this book. I have no doubt that readers will also share the sense of indebtedness which I feel to amateur recorders of the contemporary scene such as D. W. K. Jones, W. Noel Jackson, the late J. F. Higham, Charles Klapper and others whose work I have been able to draw upon for the majority of the illustrations which I needed. Finally I have included some of my own photographs, their quality much flattered by the skill of Nigel Curtis of Alcester. Having in most cases been taken after the war, these lack the period appeal of prewar shots, but they include one taken with the five-shilling camera I was given for my 11th birthday.

Although it is not uncommon for people of my age to think that things are not what they were, in the case of London Transport this is sadly true. The amputation of Country Area, for instance, severed links going back to the 1920s which were still perceptible in early postwar years. Country Area then had a particular fascination, with special buses which could only be seen by visiting out-of-the-way places. A ride in a country bus was an adventure, partly because if there ever was a comprehensive route map, I never saw one, and everything was more informal. Even Central Area in those days offered much more variety: there were still buses inherited from previous owners: buses with petrol engines and several types of diesel engines; preselective gearboxes of more than one type; buses with three axles, outside staircases and bodies fashioned and often individually refashioned by craftsmen in Chiswick works. I hope in this book I shall succeed in capturing for the reader some of the interest I found in these things.

Abbreviations Used in the Text

ADC	Associated Daimler Company
AEC	originally Associated Equipment Co, later a registered trade name in itself
bhp	Brake horsepower, ie the power developed by an engine on a test bed
ENSA	Entertainments National Service Association (a showbusiness organisation which took variety performances to service units during the 1939-45 war)
ESTC	East Surrey Traction Co
LGOC	London General Omnibus Co
LGCS	London General Country Services Ltd
LPTB	London Passenger Transport Board
NOTC	National Omnibus & Transport Co

1: Introduction

The history of the London bus begins in 1829, exactly a hundred years before the beginning of the period examined in detail in this book. On 4 July that year George Shillibeer began the first public service between Marylebone and the Bank with two vehicles to which he gave the name *Omnibus*.

The London General Omnibus Company was incorporated in 1856. It had originally been formed in Paris the previous year as the *Compagnie Generale des Omnibus de Londres*, of which it will be seen that the English name was an exact translation. The word General, so characteristic of French company names, was used as a trade name, its use continuing on buses even into London Transport days. Being better financed than previous operators of buses in London, the LGOC was able to establish garages from which a comprehensive network of routes could be operated, and it grew both by the development of new business and the acquisition of competitors. By the dawn of the motorbus era at the turn of the century a commanding majority of the buses operating in London belonged to the LGOC.

By this time a new form of street transport had appeared on the scene, the electric tramway. The growth of electric street tramways in Britain took place mainly between 1890 and 1910. In London, however, rather an unusual pattern resulted from the decision of the cities of London and Westminster and the boroughs of Kensington, St Marylebone and some others not to allow through routes to traverse their boundaries. A consequence was that although a quite extensive municipal network grew up in north and northeast and another in south and southeast London, until the Kingsway subway was built in 1906 the only connection between them was over Putney or Kingston Bridge and company-owned tracks in the northern and western suburbs. This pattern left a very profitable market to the operators of buses.

The thing which arrested the expansion of street tramways was the advent of the motorbus. In this matter the LGOC was not a significant pioneer, although by 1905 it had one garage (Cricklewood) operating motor-buses exclusively; these were of Büssing (German) and de Dion Bouton (French) manufacture. However, the first of two

events which were to change the course of transport history took place on 1 July 1908 when the LGOC took over the London Motor Omnibus Co, which not only operated a fleet of motorbuses under the name Vanguard but had facilities for building them at its works in Black Horse Road, Walthamstow.

The second historic event, which followed three and a half years later on 1 January 1912, was the takeover of the LGOC by the Underground Group. The Underground Group had risen to prominence and prosperity with the building and operation of the deep-bored underground railways in London, and it already owned the London United Tramways. It was probably the only company on the London Transport scene with the financial muscle to take over the LGOC.

The General Manager of the Underground Group was Albert Stanley, who as Lord Ashfield was later to become the first Chairman of the London Passenger Transport Board. Under his leadership the new proprietors were quick to see the potential of the facility for the design and building of motor vehicle chassis which the LGOC had acquired with the Vanguard business. On 13 June, less than six months after the acquisition of the LGOC, the vehicle building subsidiary was registered as a separate company with the name The Associated Equipment Company. AEC continued to be a subsidiary of the Underground Group until the formation of London Transport in 1933, whereupon it was floated as an independent company and received its own quotation on the London Stock Exchange. A link with its origins survived in the company's telegraphic address, Vangastow, until the end of its separate existence in the 1960s.

Most readers of this book will be familiar with the famous General B-type bus which first appeared in 1910. Enough of these buses had been produced by the outbreak of war in August 1914 to allow the last horse buses to be withdrawn, reportedly so that the Army could have the horses. Production of the B-type continued intermittently throughout the war, with some going straight to Army service. In its layout the B-type bus strongly resembled the later horse buses, with a saloon having 16 inward-facing longitudinal seats approached from a platform at the rear which was reached by two steps from the road. From the platform a staircase ascended to the open-top deck, which had 18 forward-facing seats in pairs. The driver sat under a full width canopy in front of the saloon, with the bonnet containing the engine in front of him. The seats on the upper deck were wooden slatted, whereas those in the lower saloon were upholstered with horsehair. The two decks were still respectively referred to as inside and outside (or 'on top') by busmen a generation later. Another link with horse bus days

to survive until the 1930s which the sharp-eyed reader may be able to make out in some of the illustrations in this book was the LGOC transfer for recording the axle weights, which were still given as FAW and HAW (fore-axle weight and hind-axle weight).

Civilian production of the B-type was resumed with the return of peace in 1919. However, it was shortly superseded by a new model, the K-type, in which the driving position was placed alongside instead of behind the engine, establishing the forward control layout with a half cab which was to be characteristic of most buses in Britain for the next 40 years. In the K-type as well as utilising the additional space for the saloon, in which the seating was now transverse, the top deck was carried forward part way over the driver's canopy with the result that the seating capacity went up to 46. The S-type, which appeared in 1921, was a longer version of the K-type, with a seating capacity of 54. The wheelbase of the S-type was 14ft 11in, and the overall length 24ft 8in. In the K- and S-types, which still employed the sandwich frame construction (a sawn timber board between flat steel flitches) used in the B-type, the platform was reached from road level with the aid of a single intermediate step. Production of the K- and S-types continued side by side; some of the later K-types were single-deckers on pneumatic tyres, the first buses thus equipped to enter LGOC service. However, the restriction to an overall width of 7ft 2in on which the Public Carriage Office insisted for double-deck vehicles operating within the Metropolitan Police District precluded the use of any but solid tyres, and the frame height any but an open top deck. There was however, a 'provincial' version of the double-deck S-type built to a width of 7ft 5in (or 7ft 6in) which ran on pneumatic tyres, and quite a number of these, known as PS-type, were included in the buses which the LGOC provided for its associate the East Surrey Traction Co.

From the foregoing description it will be appreciated that the design of bus chassis had not yet diverged greatly from that of goods vehicles. This, however was to change with the NS-type, the first of which was built in 1923. In the NS-type the frame members were flanged steel pressings, which were cranked sharply down behind the engine to allow a much lower floor level. The new mechanical feature which made this possible was a double reduction rear axle, in which the hubs each incorporated a ring gear which was driven by a pinion on the end of each half shaft. The middle portion of the axle was thus at a lower level than the hubs and although there was still a central worm drive differential, the worm wheel was much smaller because of the secondary gearing between it and the hubs. As the NS-type lasted until 1937, I can just remember the growling noise which issued from these axles. Interestingly, double reduction axles with a dropped central portion were to reappear in the 1950s when the floor levels of double-deck buses took another dive. In the NS-type, although there was still a step between the platform and the saloon there was none between the platform and road level. The type letters thus stood for 'no step'; they were also said to stand for *nulli secundus*. As to the latter interpretation, I will only say that the people I met at Chiswick a generation later are remembered more for a robust practical competence than for any pretensions to scholarship in Latin.

In the NS-type the wheelbase was 15ft 6in and the overall length 24ft 11in, effectively the maximum then permissible for a double-deck bus. However, the seating capacity, 52, was less than the 54 of the S-type. This was because the lower floor and ceiling of the saloon were not matched by a lower driving position, and it was thus not possible to carry the upper deck forward over the cab canopy.

The introduction of the K-, S- and NS-types coincided with the building and commissioning of Chiswick works. The LGOC's previous works at Holloway had lacked adequate capacity to turn out enough bodies for the B-type, some of which had accordingly been built by outside contractors (one of whom was as far away as Scotland). The first priority at Chiswick when work began in August 1920 was the completion of a new body shop, which began turning out bodies in March 1921. The next facility to be completed was the overhaul works, commissioned the following August. This began operation in October 1924 and for the next three years NS-type chassis for the LGOC were built up at Chiswick from sets of parts supplied by AEC. This arrangement was made to relieve pressure on the latter's Walthamstow works, which was now becoming rather cramped for the output at the level to which it had risen.

The period during which NS-type chassis were assembled at Chiswick spanned two major developments. The lower floor of the NS-type introduced the possibility of fitting a roof and windows to the upper deck within the constraints of permissible height and the tilt test. Although this possibility was demonstrated to the Public Carriage Office with the first bus completed, in 1923, it was not until 1925 that the latter agreed to allow a batch of new buses to be placed in service with covered top decks. In the light of the experience thus gained, approval was given the following year for covered tops to be fitted to all buses of the NS-type, new and existing. The second major development was the fitting of pneumatic tyres. This necessitated an increase in overall width from 7ft 2in to 7ft 5in, which the Public Carriage Office was reluctant to allow but eventually did in 1927. In both cases conversion programmes were mounted at Chiswick although it took several years to

convert the whole fleet. In the final batches of 50 and six NS-type buses, the chassis for which were built at the new Southall factory in 1928, the bodies were built out to the 7ft 5in width.

Except in the respects which have been mentioned the chassis specification of the NS-type did not break new ground. The engine was the same four-cylinder side-valve unit of 108mm bore×140mm stroke with splash lubrication which had been used in the S-type, and the majority of LGOC examples employed the same three-speed chain-driven gearbox with dog clutch engagement. The clutch was of the cone type and the brakes operated on the rear wheels only. The NS-type replaced the B-type, the last of which ran in 1927.

The Public Carriage Office which has been mentioned was, and still is, a department of the Metropolitan Police. One of the functions assigned by Parliament to the Commissioner of Police for the Metropolis in the Metropolitan Police Act was the regulation of public carriages plying for hire on the streets of London, including authority to approve their design. Probably the best known manifestation of this function to the public at large is the design of the London taxicab, which is as it is largely because of Public Carriage Office requirements in such matters as headroom and turning circle. However, the Public Carriage Office is also

Above:
LGOC B, K, S and NS-type buses at Chiswick, 1924, showing the evolution of driving position and platform height. *LT U1750*

able to stipulate certain requirements affecting the design and operation of buses within the Metropolitan Police District. Generally these have taken the form of being more stringent than the Construction and Use Regulations which apply to the Kingdom at large. An example is a tighter turning circle; when I was at AEC, in the early 1950s, RT chassis for London Transport had to turn in 56ft between kerbs whereas provincial double-deck chassis were allowed 60ft, and for quite a long time London Transport chassis had to be fitted with tyres of, in effect, obsolete design until some relaxation was allowed in this requirement.

In the 1920s the Public Carriage Office licensed buses for service within the Metropolitan Police District for 12 months at a time. At the conclusion of 12 months the buses had to be presented for relicensing in a completely overhauled condition. A new licence could be refused for dented panels or any imperfections of paintwork. The overhaul method for which Chiswick works was planned was a defensive answer to this position. Removal of the body allowed the chassis to be stripped and rebuilt with new units on an assembly line not unlike that at the factory where it had been built. However, because the body could not be dealt with by such methods — for one thing time was needed to allow paint to dry — a

float of spare bodies was kept for all the principal types of chassis which were regarded as standard, so that after overhaul a chassis received a suitable overhauled body which had been made ready in advance and not the one which it had carried when it came into the works. Because the identity of the vehicle resided in the chassis this practice enabled buses to be overhauled with only a day out of service, at a time when the cost of the licence was a significant part of the total cost of running a bus. In the early 1930s the usual LGOC practice was to build one spare body for a batch of 50 chassis or three for a batch of 100 chassis. With the approach of the London Passenger Transport Act the overhaul period was extended to 18 months and later in the 1930s to two years, whereupon the number of spare bodies built was reduced to approximately one for 100 chassis, but the larger float of bodies held for the earlier types was to stand London Transport in good stead during the 1939-45 war when many bus bodies were damaged or destroyed by enemy air attack.

The LGOC was immensely methodical in practically everything it did. Chassis were identified by the type serial number, known as the bonnet number; within batches these were usually in sequence with the manufacturer's chassis number. In later days at least, both these numbers were engraved on a

Above:
During their lives the NS-type buses were (with a few exceptions) converted to covered tops, pneumatic tyres and fitted with windscreens. Between 1933 and 1937 they were replaced by the STL-type, four examples of which can be seen in this line-up at Kensal Rise in May 1936. STL1115 (nearest the camera) has an early example of the STL11-type body with tubular aluminium seats. *LT 22072*

brass plate fixed to the frame before it was put on the assembly line at the factory. Registration numbers, although allocated by London County Council in batches of 100 or 200 (occasionally 400) were until 1938 usually applied in the order in which new chassis were received at Chiswick, although there were occasionally batches of buses in which all three numbers were in sequence. Bodies each had a separate number. A batch of body numbers would be allocated when a sanction for a new batch of buses was approved, although sometimes a sanction would cover spare bodies only, usually after a previous sanction for chassis and bodies had included none. Appendix 1 shows the correlation of known LGOC sanctions and body numbers for a period spanning the years 1929 to 1933, and Appendix 2 similar information for London Transport vehicle purchases between 1933 and 1939.

During the later 1920s things at AEC went through rather an unsettled period. In July 1926 the formation of a joint company to market the bus chassis produced by AEC and the Daimler Co of Coventry, known as

the Associated Daimler Co, was announced. This was to be based at Southall where AEC had just bought a green field site for a new factory to replace the Walthamstow works which was now clearly too small. The registered office of the joint company, however, was at 55 Broadway, SW1, and its Chairman was Lord Ashfield. Although the joint company was intended to be only a marketing organisation, it was decided that it needed a Chief Engineer and Laurence Pomeroy of the Daimler Co was appointed to this post. AEC continued to have its own Chief Engineer, Charles Edwards, who until June 1928 still had his design office at Walthamstow. One thing which Daimler were able to bring to the joint company was a six-cylinder engine, of 35hp RAC rating, 97×130mm bore and stroke, with sleeve-valves. At the beginning of 1927 AEC had no six-cylinder engine of its own. There was also a smaller Daimler six-cylinder sleeve-valve engine which was used in some lighter single-deck models, but these play no part in this narrative.

In the early part of 1927 AEC was engaged in designing, in great haste apparently, the

LS-type six-wheeled chassis for the LGOC. The haste, according to Alan Townsin in *Blue Triangle*, was because the LGOC wanted to get a six-wheeled bus into service before any of the independents who were working with Guy and Karrier. The attractions of three-axle buses were that they could be built up to a length limit of 30ft and also that they qualified for a much more generous gross weight limit. Two-axle double-deckers were at that time restricted to 25ft and a gross weight limit of 9½ tons. A range of pressed steel disc wheels of 20in nominal diameter was now available with a corresponding range of high pressure pneumatic tyres, of which the 36×8 size was rated at two tons, so that six of these tyres on a three-axle bus had a carrying capacity equal to the gross weight limit of 12 tons. These wheels were smaller than those used on the NS with pneumatic tyres, and for this reason in the design of the LS-type the dropped-centre type of axle was dispensed with in favour of single-reduction worm axles, both of which were driven through an intermediate or third differential. However, the differentials, with the larger worm wheels needed to accommodate a reduction of 8.25 or 10.33:1 in one step, were central and so the lower saloon gangway height was inevitably still some 29 or 30in above ground level. This was perhaps the most significant of many respects in which the design of the LS-type was inferior to that of the Leyland Titan which appeared later the same year. In the Titan, a two-axle double-decker chassis, the differential was offset so that it came under the footstools of the longitudinal seats over the nearside rear wheels and the gangway was over a plain portion of the axle. As the tyres were also smaller, 34×7, the lower saloon floor level in the Titan was a full five inches lower than it was in the LS-type. Also the LS-type, like the NS, originally had brakes on the rear wheels only whereas the Titan had brakes on both front and rear wheels (by mechanical linkage from the vacuum servo, that to the front wheels passing through the hollow kingpins).

The first chassis built, LS1, which was licensed in June 1927, was built with the Daimler sleeve-valve engine, with which a single plate clutch and an axle ratio of 10.33:1 were used. However LS2, licensed in July, was delivered with a six-cylinder AEC side-valve engine of 108mm bore by 140mm stroke, the same dimensions as the four-cylinder unit used in the NS-type. This engine, AEC unit number A121, was appreciably larger in terms of swept volume than the Daimler engine and with it an axle ratio of 8.25:1 was used. It also drove through a single-plate clutch, an advance on previous AEC practice. With both engines a separately mounted four-speed crash gearbox was used, whereas the gearbox in the Titan, although similar in being of the four-speed crash type, was mounted as a unit with the engine, an arrangement of which minimised

the primary shaft inertia and so made gearchanging quicker if not significantly easier.

No more buses of the LS-type were to enter LGOC service in 1927. There was trouble with the Public Carriage Office, which objected to the design of the inside-stair body and insisted on the bodies of both LS1 and LS2 being converted to an outside staircase design before it would allow any more LS-type buses to be licensed. LS3-12 were completed and licensed a few at a time between February 1928 and January 1929. Apart from LS6, which was a single-decker (and originally had electric transmission), these buses were completed with outside-stair double-deck bodies originally seating 70. Only LS3 and LS12, the latter by three months the last to enter service, originally had AEC A121 engines; the other eight all originally had Daimler sleeve-valve engines. However, by the end of 1929 all the nine buses which were originally equipped with sleeve-valve engines had been given 100×130mm overhead camshaft petrol engines of the new type designed by Rackham for the Reliance chassis (we shall come to these shortly) and the three AEC-engined examples were similarly treated in January and February 1930. The axle ratio used in all cases was now 8.25:1. The LS chassis went through further vicissitudes in LPTB days, acquiring 110mm bore engines, LT-type front axles with brakes and worm and nut steering boxes before being finally withdrawn in 1937. Four of them were then converted to breakdown tenders and survived in this form until 1951.

Returning to 1927, however, the model 802 chassis (the AEC designation of the LS-type) was taken on board as an Associated Daimler product. Construction of 20 chassis was authorised, of which 12 went to the LGOC; two were completed with LGOC-built bodies as the famous 104-seaters for ferrying AEC personnel between Walthamstow and Southall, for which purpose they could run on trade plates and were exempt from the Construction & Use Regulations governing buses which plied for hire, and six were completed as demonstrators. One of these was shown on the Associated Daimler stand at the Commercial Motor Show held at Olympia in November 1927 at which the Leyland Titan also made its first public appearance. However, whereas the Titan was destined to be the forerunner of thousands, the Associated Daimler Vehicle failed to attract a single order. The LGOC's LS3-12 were the last 10 of the 20 chassis built, and in fact the entry 'ex AD Co.' on the LGOC rolling stock card for LS12 was the last — or one of the last — such entries ever to be made. This was because, not surprisingly, the commercial failure of the LS-type produced strains within the AEC-Daimler marriage from which it was never to recover. One reason that Daimler had entered into it was to gain a share in the double-deck bus market for which, it appeared to the Daimler management, its six-cylinder sleeve-valve engine should have been suitable. However, by the second anniversary of the formation of ADC, in July 1928, only one order, apart from the LS fiasco, for 50 double-deck buses had been placed by the LGOC and these did not have Daimler engines. Deciding that enough was enough, Daimler resolved that it would do better in the bus market on its own, and on its own it went, taking Pomeroy and the sleeve-valve engine with it.

This left AEC with the Southall factory but with a serious lack of competitive modern products to make in it. Lord Ashfield was quick to take in this situation and he solved the problem in a characteristically imaginative way, by hiring George John Rackham, the man who had designed the Titan for Leyland. At the beginning of July 1928, Rackham became Chief Engineer of AEC, replacing Charles Edwards (who deserves to be remembered for the NS-type) and charged with the task of designing a new range of chassis, passenger and goods, to be built at Southall.

The first AEC product to bear the imprint of Rackham was the Reliance single-deck chassis, model 660, announced in the autumn of 1928. Essentially this was the current ADC 426 model — itself a facelift of the previous 416 — with an all-new six-cylinder overhead camshaft engine of 100mm bore and 130mm stroke, the design of which closely resembled the engine Rackham had designed for the Leyland Titan. By closely following his earlier design, Rackham was able to produce the new engine in an astonishingly short space of time: Alan Townsin in *Blue Triangle* tells us that the first engine was on test within

three months of Rackham's appointment at AEC. A notable and overdue innovation was the provision of pressure lubrication for both the main bearings and big ends, and the rated power of 95bhp was a 60% increase on the output of the four-cylinder side-valve engine fitted to the 426. The resulting increase in performance forced the inclusion of front-wheel brakes as a standard feature in the chassis specification, this being achieved in rather a makeshift manner with a universal joint where the camshafts which expanded the brake shoes intersected the kingpin axes. In other respects, however, the chassis was practically unaltered, retaining the worm and sector steering, separate four-speed gearbox with right hand change, fully floating axle with central worm drive and even the cone clutch of the previous model. It was not intended as anything but a stopgap and as such it served its purpose. The last Reliance chassis was produced in 1931. Some 45 Reliances came into the ownership of London Transport in due course.

Rackham next set about designing a complete new range of passenger chassis incorporating practically nothing from any previous AEC model except the six-cylinder overhead camshaft engine he had just designed for the Reliance. This now acquired a bellhousing, as the new models incorporated unit construction of engine and gearbox between which there was a single plate clutch. The power output of the 6.1-litre 100mm×130mm engine, 95bhp at 2,400rpm, was unchanged from the Reliance. The gearbox, unit number D119, provided four forward speeds with sliding mesh engagement of all the indirect ratios. The rear axle was a new design, of the semi-floating type with the 7in centres

Right:
The most significant chassis of the Associated Daimler period was the ADC 416 single-deck model, some of which were fitted with coach bodies by the LGOC. In March 1930 to meet a need for coaches to work the new Watford-Golders Green and Watford-Charing Cross services, nine of these exchanged bodies with Reliances which had been built with bus bodies for the Watford Area services in June 1929. These bodies foreshadowed the design produced later that year for the T-type and pioneered the use of a roller blind destination box. However, in accordance with the general practice in the 1920s the driver's cab was mounted separately on the chassis and thus the 416 seen here in LGCS days still has its original open structure.
D. W. K. Jones

worm drive differential offset to the near-side, resembling the unit Rackham had designed for the Titan in these respects. The front axle was also a new design, with hollow kingpins through which passed the mechanical linkage from the cross-shaft behind the servo amidships to the front brakes. This too was a repeat of the arrangement Rackham had used in the Titan. However, in the Regent and Regal, as the new double and single chassis were called, Rackham achieved a much more compact front end design, in which the radiator was at the extreme front of the chassis (the protruding starter dog being disregarded for purposes of compliance with the Construction & Use Regulations). The effective bonnet length from the extreme front of the chassis to the bulkhead behind the engine was a full 6in less than the equivalent dimension in the Titan. Coupled with the elegant new AEC radiator design with parallel sides and a central division extending downwards from the blue-enamelled AEC triangle, this helped to create a much more modern appearance compared with the rather vintage sports-car look of the original Leyland Titan. One wonders if this was something forced on Rackham by the conservatism of some of the Leyland directors; if it was it was a curious step backwards from the original model PLSC Lion. Leyland was to redesign the front end of its Titan and Tiger passenger chassis in 1933 on the pattern of the AEC Regent and Regal; in these it survived virtually without alteration for the life of the model run, which extended until 1947.

The new AEC model range announced in June 1929 consisted of the Regent double-decker chassis, model 661, which had a wheelbase of 15ft 6½in for an intended overall length of 25ft, 36×8 tyres on 20in dia wheels and a standard axle ratio of 6.25:1; and the Regal single-decker chassis, model 662, which had a wheelbase of 17ft 0in for alternative overall lengths of 26ft and 27ft; 26ft seems to have been the longest overall length permitted by the Public Carriage Office for buses licensed for service in London at that time, but in other parts of the country a length of 27ft 6in was permissible. The original Leyland Tiger TS1 was designed to this length and the 27ft long Regal offered the same body space, thanks to the more compact front end design. The wheelbase of the Regal was, however, a foot longer than the Reliance and this made it difficult to incorporate a rear sliding door within the 26ft length limit. The Regal in its original form used 38×8¼ tyres on 22in wheels; the standard axle ratio was 6.25:1, the same as the Regent. Both models used a Marles cam and roller steering box.

To cater primarily for, or more exactly in the hope of attracting, LGOC interest there were also two versions of a three-axle chassis known as the Renown. The first of these was model 663, with a wheelbase of 16ft 6in measured from the front axle to the rear bogie centre pin, for an overall length of 27ft. This was the model in which the LGOC was interested for double-deck use, but there was also a longer version, model 664, with a wheelbase of 18ft 7in to cater for an overall length of 30ft, the maximum permissible for either single or double-deckers with three axles. After an early intention of the LGOC to order two maximum capacity double-deckers was abandoned, 200 long-wheelbase Renown chassis were ordered by the LGOC for single-deckers in 1930-31 (although one of these was completed as an experimental double-deck coach) and this was the model for which orders for all but four Renown chassis were received during its currency from sources other than the LGOC and the LPTB. In the Renown a bogie with single wheels was used at the rear; in this both axles were driven with a three-differential arrangement which equalised the torque transmitted to all four wheels. Unlike the LS-type, the differentials were offset. As in the Regent and Regal, the rear axles were of the semi-floating type. Torque reaction was taken by a torque blade fitted between the axles. The front end of the chassis was identical with the Regent; there was, however, an important difference in the brakes. The first chassis built, 663001, which went to the LGOC in June 1929 to become LT1, originally had no front brakes, but all subsequent Renown chassis had front brakes which were operated by separate slave servos mounted on a cross member adjacent to the main servo amidships. This arrangement proved to give a much more effective and better balanced braking system than the single servo and uncompensated mechanical linkage originally used in the Regent and Regal chassis and it was later adopted as standard in the latter until in turn displaced by the Lockheed hydraulic system. Many of the earlier chassis were converted to the triple servo system by operators, including the LGOC and Tillings.

Despite initial uncertainty, support from the LGOC coupled with its good design were to secure for the Renown a commercial success which far exceeded that enjoyed by any other British three-axled bus chassis. It was later to provide the basis of the three-axle trolleybuses built by both AEC and Leyland for London Transport and other users. Primarily to cater for these, AEC redesigned the bogie in 1934 with fully floating axles and larger (8in centres) worm drive units. The Renown was supplied as standard with two 25gal fuel tanks, one on each sidemember, whereas the Regent and Regal had a single 35gal tank which was fitted on the offside as standard. In the Renown in its original form with 100mm bore engine the LGOC used an axle ratio of 8.33:1 in double-deck versions and 6.75:1 in single-deck.

Understandably, the fiasco of the LS-type and the Associated Daimler debacle also had an effect at certain levels in the LGOC itself. Naturally it was remembered that the NS-type had been assembled at Chiswick with complete satisfaction for three years, and in the mood prevailing in the middle of 1928 it did not, to some minds at least, seem an enormous step from this to designing and building complete chassis at Chiswick. At this time all that was known about Rackham was that he had designed the Leyland Titan, and the facts that this bus had not only seen off the LS-type but that examples were already in service with some of the pirates, enabling them to offer the travelling public standards of refinement and performance which no LGOC bus could match, touched on some sensitive places. Whether or not he had a letter of appointment from Lord Ashfield in his pocket, it was not a foregone conclusion that such a man ought to be entrusted with the LGOC's business.

Some thoughts such as these clearly underlay a fascinating sanction, No 24/918, raised by the LGOC probably in the early summer of 1929. This authorised the construction of six three-axle double-deckers to be designed and built at Chiswick and known as CC type; six two-axle single-deckers to be designed and built at Chiswick and known as CB-type; two maximum-capacity double-deckers on AEC Renown long-wheelbase chassis; an AEC Regent chassis for use as such in the training school at Chiswick (this was to have the number ST517), and a double-deck bus on AEC Regent chassis with an enclosed-staircase body of new design, which was to have the number ST1.

It is a pity that we do not know the date of this sanction. The LGOC was privy to the plans of AEC and the availability of the Renown chassis in two lengths is disclosed, as well as that of the Regent. A start was to be made on the design and development of chassis to be built at Chiswick. However, the two types authorised do not include a two-axle double-decker, although this may have been envisaged as a later possibility, perhaps to be known as CA-type. In view of the time it will take to get design, development and manufacture of the CB and CC-types under way, the purchase of a further 500 ST-type buses on AEC Regent chassis is clearly contemplated to follow approval of the prototype ST1, plus 15 for the LGOC services based on Watford operated by the National Omnibus & Transport Co. The background to this last arrangement will be explained shortly.

In accordance with usual LGOC practice a batch of 16 body numbers was reserved to match the 16 chassis covered by this sanction. These were Nos 10478 to 10493 inclusive. At this time LGOC body numbers allocated had reached 10227. The intervening 250 body numbers had been set aside for buses to be built on AEC chassis, the intention to order which had been conveyed to AEC. It was reported in the press in August 1929 that the LGOC had ordered 270 AEC chassis of the new type (meaning the Regent, Regal and Renown). Although this was not an exact statement of the contractual position at that time, the figure of 270 was correct, as it included 15 Regents for the National services for which body numbers had not yet been allocated and five Regal private hire coaches which would receive body numbers in a separate series, as well as 50 Regals, 50 double-deck model 663 Renowns, 50 single-deck model 664 Renowns and 100 Regents for ordinary LGOC bus services. As we shall shortly see, it was April 1931 before all these were in service.

Some blanks were destined to arise in this batch of 16 body numbers. One was inevitable because a number had been allocated to the instruction chassis which was never intended to have a body — a straightforward mistake. The sanction was also destined to be pruned, the number of CC-type buses being reduced from six to four, the CB-type from six to three and two maximum capacity Renowns axed completely. This was probably not until some time in 1930, as it was not in time to prevent five CC-type bodies being completed.

As we shall see in the chapter after next, a blank also arose in the batch of 250 bodies reserved for AEC chassis. This came about because LT1 was given a body which was already in hand, and consequently only 49 bodies were built within the reserved batch for LT-type double-deckers instead of the scheduled 50.

We do not know how much work had been done at AEC on the first two long-wheelbase Renown chassis before they were cancelled, but in the event they were completed for an order received from Warrington Corporation in 1930.

The type letters ST, T and LT were chosen by the LGOC to denote the AEC Regent, Regal and Renown models. The rationale of this choice seems to have been that these three models constituted a family of which in terms of overall length the Regent at 25ft was the shortest and the Renown, whether at 27ft or 30ft, was the longest, the Regal, at 26ft, being intermediate. The type letter R had already been used for the Reliance and the famous S-type buses of 1921-23 were still in service. At the time this choice was made the distinctly odd decision to number the Chiswick chassis in the LT and T series had probably not been taken.

Whilst the foregoing is an outline of events affecting chassis manufacture up to the middle of 1929, it may also be helpful to outline the relationships which existed between the LGOC and its subsidiaries and associates at that time. Chief among the associates was Thomas Tilling Ltd, the second largest bus operator in London. Tilling was tolerated by the LGOC because under an agreement reached in 1914 (there were also subsidiary agreements at later dates) it paid its receipts into a common pool and as a result it was allowed to operate certain routes on behalf of the LGOC for which the latter provided the buses. At the beginning of the 1930s there were 114 such buses, 102 double-deck and 12 single-deck. Tilling owned a works at Peckham and a body factory at Lewisham, but the garages from which the company worked during the later years of its independent existence, at Croydon, Catford and Bromley, were leased from the LGOC.

Another associate was Overground Ltd, whose original depot was in Camden Town but which (following a fire) became a subsidiary of the LGOC and tenant of its garage at Potters Bar, from which they worked into central London on Route 134 (Potters Bar-Pimlico). The LGOC also operated buses on behalf of the Metropolitan Electric Tramways Co, by this time an Underground Group Associate.

The LGOC, which had a working agreement with the East Surrey Traction Co of Reigate dating from July 1921, acquired a controlling interest in that company in June 1929. Here again the LGOC provided the buses for what were called the joint services and certain other services which the LGOC transferred to the ESTC. Following the acquisition of control the LGOC placed

Autocar Services Ltd of Tunbridge Wells, in which it had acquired a controlling interest in February 1929, under the ESTC for management purposes although the two undertakings were kept separate. Autocar became wholly owned by the LGOC in August 1929; however, Autocar vehicles were not given LGOC fleet numbers or body numbers whereas buses provided for operation by the East Surrey but owned by the LGOC, although numbered in the ESTC fleet, had LGOC body numbers.

North of the River Thames the LGOC had a working agreement with the National Omnibus & Transport Co, also dating from July 1921, under which the latter operated the LGOC's services in the Watford District (which included St Albans and Luton) using buses provided by the LGOC. These services included a joint route to Chesham with the Amersham & District Motor Bus and Haulage Co in which the LGOC acquired half the ordinary capital in August 1929. A similar arrangement with the NOTC was made at Hertford following the acquisition of the Hertford & District bus company in 1924. There was also an agreement with the Thames Valley Traction Co covering services based on Windsor, Staines and High Wycombe and another with the Aldershot & District Traction Co covering those in the Guildford-Woking area.

Below:
LS12, the last LS-type bus to be built, at Hyde Park Corner in 1930. *LT U5576*

2: Organisational Developments, 1930-35

In 1930 the LGOC started the coach services which were to be incorporated in July as Green Line Coaches Ltd. These grew out of a service begun in December 1929 between Golders Green and Watford using Reliances bought earlier that year for private hire and tours. These had bodies with folding canvas roofs and swing doors; vehicles of this description were obviously not ideal for a fixed-interval limited-stop service, which was what the new route was, but they happened to be available because it was winter and they were delicensed.

Before any further development of such services could take place it was clearly necessary to acquire some more suitable vehicles. There was an obvious choice of chassis in the newly-introduced AEC Regal, 50 of which were just being delivered for new LGOC buses in the closing months of 1929. Not surprisingly, an ideal design of body was not achieved at the first attempt. The first body produced for the Green Line services (for which one of the bus chassis was appropriated) had a fixed metal-panelled roof, half-drop windows and a floor high enough to allow the use of forward facing seats over the wheel arches, reached by two internal steps. For passenger access, however, this body still had a swing door behind the rear wheel which, it was shortly realised, was not what was wanted for the new services. With its 17ft wheelbase, when built to an overall length of 26ft the rear overhang of the Regal was too short to allow an entrance with a sliding door of acceptable width. This problem was avoided in the 150 vehicles which followed by recessing the door so that although of the hinged type, it opened within the body. After this it was realised that a better layout could be achieved by moving the entrance to the front where there were no constraints on the width of sliding door which could be used. This layout was adopted for 100 vehicles delivered early in 1931 and all subsequent coaches for the next 20 years.

In the early stages the services envisaged were between the fringes of the LGOC empire and a central terminal point and a coach station was hurriedly built at Poland Street, near Oxford Circus. Not all of the services used this, however; other termini used included Marble Arch, Charing Cross and Aldgate. In many cases these locations were already used by earlier established but generally less frequent services operated by associated companies of the LGOC such as Amersham & District, East Surrey and Autocar. Coaches of the first order were painted in the liveries of all these companies before Green Line Coaches Ltd was formed in July 1930 and began to assert its corporate image.

Within the Metropolitan Police District the Commissioner of Police had power to regulate bus and coach services under the London Traffic Act of 1924 and the police shortly began complaining of congestion being caused by coaches in the vicinity of the London terminal points. The solution adopted as the Green Line network expanded was to introduce new routes which operated, as far as was practical, right across London without a layover in the centre. The principal exceptions to this policy were the services to the east and northeast of London, which terminated at Aldgate on weekdays, and later, routes taken over from other operators with licences under the 1930 Road Traffic Act such as the Queen Line service between King's Cross and Baldock. Services in the latter category were generally to be integrated into the cross-town network within a year or two and the Poland Street coach station was disposed of before the formation of the London Passenger Transport Board in 1933.

The 1930 Road Traffic Act introduced licensing for bus and coach services outside the Metropolitan Police District from the beginning of March 1931. This gave additional urgency to the expansion of the Green Line network and the 150 27-seat coaches placed in traffic in 1930 were followed in great haste by a further 100 (of the improved design seating 30, with a sliding door at the front) licensed in January and February 1931. The object was to get services established to be able to claim sitting tenant status in applications for licences. The rolling stock cards for some of these vehicles revealed some unlikely stabling points: Metcalfe Engineering Co, Romford; L. Prime, Motor Engineers, Hitchin, and the AEC works at Southall, though there was a special reason for this last choice for three of the four vehicles based there. One called Slough (PH) was presumably an LGOC depot for private hire coaches. Otherwise the Green Line vehicles worked mainly from National, Amersham, East Surrey and Autocar garages, though specific Green Line garages were established at Watford and later at Romford.

At the beginning of 1932 the LGOC acquired the remaining capital of the East Surrey Traction Co in which it had previously only held a controlling interest. The company's name was thereupon changed to London General Country Services Ltd

and, due notice having been given to the National Omnibus & Transport Co, from 7 April that year LGCS began to operate the services based on Watford and Ware which the NOTC had previously worked as an agent. LGCS now served the whole of what later became the Country Area of the LPTB; however, the headquarters remained at Bell Street, Reigate and the business of Autocar continued to be kept separate although controlled from the same address. LGCS was given a kind of launching present in the shape of 25 new buses, 23 double-deck and two single-deck, the bodies for which were built at Chiswick in August 1932.

On 29 July 1932 the Green Line business was transferred to London General Country Services; before this however, on 11 June, while the former was still administered from Chiswick, 16 former East Surrey touring coaches were transferred into Green Line ownership, as a result of which they received LGOC body numbers, as had the coaches acquired in February with the business of Buck's Expresses. After the Green Line business was transferred to LGCS a different process took place which resulted not only in these vehicles but also 21 touring coaches belonging to Autocar being numbered in the Green Line fleet. However, the latter remained the property

of Autocar and passed with that undertaking and its other vehicles to Maidstone and District at the formation of London Transport on 1 July 1933. Excepted from this arrangement was the coach route previously worked by Autocar between Tunbridge Wells and London (continuing to Chertsey and Woking) which passed to London Transport, as did the coach station and garage used by this service in Tunbridge Wells.

The use, and extension, of LGOC bonnet numbers for coaches by LGCS is surprising. The new organisation did not consider it necessary to identify buses other than by their registration numbers, and this practice continued into LPTB days until 25 February 1935 when the engineering administration of Country Area was transferred from Reigate to Chiswick (whereupon some duplication which had arisen came to light). The fleet numbers of former East Surrey buses were allowed to lapse; however, any which had once been numbered by the LGOC, including five T-type and two ST-type buses transferred to the East Surrey in April 1931, 15 ST-type built for the National services at Watford in 1930 and four for those at Ware in 1931, resumed these numbers in 1935. LGCS was run much more like a small provincial bus company

Above:
The original Green Line coach station at Poland Street, near Oxford Circus, February 1931. Note the difference in roof profile between the 1930 and 1931 series coach bodies. *LT U8081*

and, for an author working mainly from records kept at Chiswick at least, the lack of comparable information dating from the period when these vehicles were maintained at Reigate leaves some gaps in our knowledge.

A particularly strange matter is that five private hire coaches bought by the LGOC in 1930 were originally numbered T154-150 in reverse sequence with their registration numbers GF479-483. Having been included in the Green Line fleet after the formation of Green Line Coaches Ltd they were transferred to LGCS with the rest of the fleet in 1932, and during their time with LGCS the bonnet numbers were switched so that they were henceforth in sequence with the registration numbers. (The latter continued, of course, to be tied to the AEC chassis numbers). In this case these vehicles, which were classified as charabancs by the LGOC, may not have displayed their bonnet

Right:

T26, one of five LGOC T-type buses transferred to the East Surrey Traction Co in April 1931, at Erith in LGCS days. Note that the original half-drop windows have been replaced by fixed glass; also the absence of a bonnet or fleet number.
J. F. Higham

Below:

T317 (LGCS numbering), one of the all-weather touring coaches bought by the ESTC in 1931, in Green Line service at Sunbury early in 1933. Bonnet numbers we used for coaches in LGCS days; in 1935 this vehicle was renumbered T401 (see view on page 72).
J. F. Higham

numbers when new, and a photograph of T151 taken in 1934 shows the bonnet number on a plate which is not of the standard LGOC pattern. One is left wondering whether the survival of the LGOC bonnet numbers of the vehicles mentioned in the previous paragraph depended on anything more than the plate originally fixed to the bonnet side.

The London Passenger Transport Board was established under the 1933 Act of the same name, with a chairman and six members appointed by the Minister of Transport, to take over the provision and operation of all public passenger transport within an area which corresponded closely with the territory formerly served by the LGOC and LGCS but excluded that served by Autocar. The first Chairman was Lord Ashfield, the former Chairman of the Underground Group (and of the LGOC). The Vice-Chairman, chosen by the Board from among its members, was Frank Pick, the former Managing Director of the LGOC, who was a whole-time member of the Board appointed by the Minister. The vesting date was 1 July 1933, on which the LGOC and the Underground Group ceased to exist as such but, as can be seen, the new organisation had a very strong LGOC flavour (as far as bus services were concerned) and, being in the driving seat on Day 1, LGOC personnel not surprisingly dominated the new organisation. No 55 Broadway, the former headquarters of the Underground Group, and Chiswick works, the engineering and maintenance centre of the LGOC, served the same respective functions for the LPTB from its inception.

The undertakings transferred to the LPTB by Parliament were listed in the Act; they included five railway companies, 14 municipally owned and three company-owned tramway undertakings and 61 independent bus operators. Whereas it was practical to transfer the railway and tramway undertakings on the vesting date, the only bus operating undertakings transferred on that date were the LGOC, the bus operations of Tilling & British Automobile Traction which were worked by the LGOC and the Watford Omnibus Co, whose acquisition by LGCS had alrady been agreed. For all the others there was a process of expropriation to be gone through, involving compensation and, generally, arbitration by an independent tribunal set up under the Act.

The next bus undertakings transferred were those of Thomas Tilling in London and the Lewis Omnibus Co in Watford, both on 1 October 1933. Both of these were sizeable operations by the respective criteria of Central and Country Areas. Of the remainder, the majority were much smaller; the operations of most of these had been transferred to the Board by the end of its first year of existence on 30 June 1934. Those that had not were mainly the strongest London independent operators — 11 of them, all sizeable undertakings —

which managed to retain their services until transfer dates between July and December 1934. The compensation for these companies had not been agreed by the time the Board published its first and second Annual Reports, which it did together on 31 October 1935.

As well as taking over the undertakings listed for transfer in the Act, the obligation placed on the Board to provide all passenger transport services within its area included powers to license the provision of such services to other operators. This was something which after the end of 1934 in practice only occurred in the Country Area. The Act provided that if the Board refused renewal of a licence, it must acquire the vehicles or business of the operator (on terms which could be fixed by the Arbitration Tribunal), and in this book mention will be found of services and vehicles which came to London Transport in this way in 1935. There were other instances as late as 1939.

In administration and engineering terms, the absorption of the services and vehicles of the independent operators was an enormous task. For a start, very few of the premises from which these undertakings — some of whom had only two or three buses — worked were retained for more than a few months. There was therefore a considerable estates operation. The buses acquired had to be allocated, in most cases, to former LGOC, LGCS or Tilling garages which in turn had to be made able to accommodate and to operate them, or, more particularly in Country Area, to new garages which had to be built.

Most of these vehicles were not of types which had previously been regarded as standard by the LGOC and this meant a serious storekeeping problem with spares. Furthermore, the vehicles when acquired were not always up to a standard which would satisfy the requirements of certification by the Public Carriage Office and this meant a lot of extra work at Chiswick. In acknowledgement of this, the Public Carriage Office relaxed its previous insistence on a complete overhaul every year to 18 months, but, as we shall see in a later chapter, this introduced its own problems in maintaining a controllable flow of work through the works during the changeover from one regime to the other.

Quite early in London Transport days a laudable attempt was made to identify variants of chassis and bodies and their mutual compatibility or lack of it for the benefit of works and garage staff. This was the introduction of engineering codes for the principal vehicle types. This took the form of an ingenious but quite easily understood classification in which each principal variation of a chassis type was given a number preceding the type letter, eg 1STL for STL1-49. A body variant was denoted by a number following, eg STL1. Thus the complete code for STL1-49 was

1STL 1; for STL 153-202, which incorporated differerences of chassis but not of body specification, the code was 2STL1, and the bodies could be interchanged between the two series of chassis.

What were considered to be minor variations of chassis were denoted by a figure preceding a stroke in front of the main code (eg 3/9STL). Similarly minor variations of bodies were denoted by a figure following a stroke after the main code. Thus the last 103 56-seat bodies built for LT501-950, which had three front destination boxes, were coded LT5/1 (in their form to fit petrol-engined crash-gearbox chassis) whereas the earlier examples with single destination boxes were LT5.

In the early days an engraved brass plate was fitted to the chassis (on the nearside dumb-iron) which gave both the chassis code and, in smaller characters, the codes of the bodies which would fit it without alteration, thus: 2LT LT3, 4, 5, 5/1. Similarly with body plates, which were fitted to the cab side above the bonnet a little way back from the windscreen. However, after an initial order of engraved plates to cater for existing vehicle types, subsequent plates were stamped and gave the chassis or body code only.

The code system probably worked at its best in the case of the LT-type, all but three of which came from the LGOC and were well documented at Chiswick. However, with the ex-LGOC T-type buses (T1-50 and 156, with six exceptions), which were coded after conversion to front entrance, the pitfalls of an excess of zeal became apparent. Two specifications, 1T and 2/1T, were established for buses with triple servo brakes according to engine bore and axle ratio; two for buses with Lockheed brakes (1/1T and 3/1T, there being only one example of the latter), whereas T43, which had originally had an eight-cylinder engine and shortened body (but had lost both in 1931) was coded 2T2. T10, which had received the shortened body, was included in 1T1.

At Reigate the transition from LGCS to the Country Area of London Transport meant little change for 20 months after the new organisation came into being. Only 14 buses were delivered during this time and these, like those taken over, were unnumbered save by their registration numbers and were lettered General, with the owner's name and address given as London Passenger Transport Board, Bell Street, Reigate. No attempt was made to convert T-type buses from rear to front entrance or either ST or T-types from single to triple servo brakes. On 25 February 1935, however, responsibility for the maintenance of Country Area vehicles was transferred to the Chief Engineer (Road Services), which meant that they were henceforth overhauled at Chiswick and record cards were again kept there.

Many of the Country Area buses were now numbered for the first time as well as being coded after a fashion. The unnumbered ST-type buses were now numbered from ST1032 upwards in strict order of their registration numbers — a procedure which had the effect of splitting the 23 Bluebirds into three batches, although two of these were contiguous. Rather touchingly, a gap was left for ST1051, which had met its end in a fire on Reigate Hill in LGCS days. The buses which had originally been numbered in the LGOC ST series reverted to their original numbers.

The numbering of the T-type buses and coaches was more haphazard. The only rational thing about it was that the coaches were all numbered first (apart, that is, from the five buses transferred from the LGOC to the ESTC with Crayford garage in April 1931, which reverted to their original numbers), but the two ex-Lewis 1930 coaches were mixed up among ex-Amersham vehicles, after which came the two Lewis coaches of 1932, followed by three buses (two from Watford Omnibus Co, one from St Albans & District) in registration number order. Then came eight ex-East Surrey buses of 1930, followed by the three front-entrance buses of 1931, after which came the other eight 1930 buses. When it was discovered that the numbers T307-318 had been duplicated, the Buck's Expresses and 10 East Surrey coaches were renumbered T391-402, leaving a rump of six East Surrey coaches of the 1931 batch numbered T319-324. It would have been better if Chiswick had swallowed its pride and renumbered the Tilling buses.

The 12 Godstone buses were numbered STL1044-1055 in order of their registration numbers, and not in sequence with their chassis numbers, as was usual Chiswick practice.

In the case of buses taken over from independent operators by London Transport which fell into the Central Area, the procedure followed was exactly the same as it had been in LGOC days. A card was raised in the rolling stock office at Chiswick and a body number was allocated — this being the next number in the body stock book formerly kept by the LGOC, and (until 1939, when a new series was begun at 1) in the same series. A bonnet number was also allocated unless the chassis was of a model not previously encountered and unlikely to be kept. Until May 1934 buses which went through the paint shop were lettered General; this may well have stiffened the resistance of some independent operators to being taken over and from June 1934 onwards all buses in both Central and Country Areas were lettered London Transport. Among the illustrations in this book examples will be found of both Central and Country Area buses lettered General and one with LPTB bonnet number and garage

plates but still in the livery and lettering of its former owner.

A point which needs to be firmly understood is that buses belonging to Country Area were subject to exactly the same procedure after responsibility for Country Area engineering was transferred to Chiswick in February 1935. This is when all country buses which had not previously carried LGOC bonnet numbers were numbered. New cards were raised at Chiswick and new body numbers allocated for all such vehicles, including ones for which old cards were still in existence from a time when they had belonged to the LGOC before being transferred to LGCS.

Apart from the 23 Bluebirds, which became 3ST4, the coding of the Country Area vehicles of the ST and T-types was haphazard in the extreme — so much so as to vitiate any value the system may have had. The code 3/1ST9/1 was applied to the six buses with lowbridge bodies originally built for the National services, which had nearside fuel tanks, and also to the two ex-Amersham buses which had offside fuel tanks. All the remaining ST-type buses were coded 2/1ST9, including examples with one servo, three servos, LGOC bodies of both the ST1/1 and ST2 types, Ransomes square-cab bodies on the model of ST1, Short Bros bodies with inside stairs and in the case of ST1139, outside stairs, and some with nearside and some with offside fuel tanks. As regards the T-type coaches, the code 7T7 was applied to T38 (which had an offside fuel tank and six-bay body with swing door) and also to T51-149, 155 and 157-206, which had nearside fuel tanks seven-bay bodies with recessed doors and the last 50 of which had triple servo brakes. The code 1/7T7/1

applied to all the front-entrance coaches T207-306, which had offside tanks, except for the three with oil engines, which were 2/7T7/1, and T232 whose totally non-standard body was only distinguished by the sub-code T7/2. The code 8T applied to both 1931 and 1930 specification Regal chassis which happened to carry 27ft long all-weather coach bodies. All the country buses T369-390 were coded 4/1T6, whether on 1930 or 1931 specification chassis and 26ft or 27ft long. However, when T369 received an ex-Green Line body from T300 it was recoded 1/7T7/1. (It is, admittedly, likely that the chassis was updated at the same time.) As applied to most of these vehicles, the code system was meaningless.

Although the code system generally worked well in application to ex-LGOC types, it had a blind spot where vehicles retained special equipment which had originally been fitted experimentally and had not been specified in the sanction for the purchase of the vehicles in question. An example was LT191-9, the first nine LT-type vehicles built with AEC-Acro oil engines. By the time the LPTB came into being the engines had been reworked to the AEC-Ri-

cardo specification and these nine chassis were given the code 4LT in common with the later vehicles built with such engines. These had been specified in the sanction for LT501-950 and codes were allocated to the bodies (two variants, LT5/3 and LT5/4) originally fitted to these chassis. However, no proper code was raised for the LT3-type bodies originally fitted to LT191-9 although these were confined to 4LT-type chassis until these vehicles were scrapped in 1948-49 and were obviously special to these chassis.

The London Passenger Transport Act was a milestone in the history of the capital whose effects were felt by ordinary people with no particular interest in buses or trains. It brought to an end competition in the supply of street transport and substituted the monolithic public corporation known as London Transport. Fortunately the Act allowed the body building facility at Chiswick of the former LGOC to continue to serve as the principal source of bodies for the buses and coaches operated by London Transport. However, the exigencies of war put an end to the production of bodies at Chiswick in 1942 and it was never resumed.

3: The LGOC ST, T and LT Types, 1929-30

Of the models in the new AEC chassis range described in Chapter 1 the Regent and Regal were aimed at the general market for buses whereas the Renown was designed to cater for interest which was largely confined to the LGOC. The first 12 Regent chassis were built as demonstrators, that is to say they were made available for potential customers to have on service trial (for periods of up to 12 months in some cases) without their having to buy them. The very first chassis, 661001, was built in the Experimental Department at Southall in February 1929 and it was sent shortly afterwards to Short Bros of Rochester to receive a 50-seat outside-stair body. Although of normal height with a central gangway upstairs, this body bore a striking resemblance to the body Rackham had designed at Leyland for the first Titan, and we may therefore assume that Rackham dictated its general design. The completed vehicle was demonstrated at the conference of the Municipal Tramways & Transport Association in June; however, by the end of that month seven more chassis had been completed with similar bodies. One of these, 661008, was

delivered to the LGOC at Chiswick on 2 July and was licensed with a registration number (UU6610) from the LGOC's then current reserved batch. The LGOC, however, allocated it to its East Surrey associate, with which it entered service from Reigate on 4 July. The significance of this date, the centenary of the inauguration of Shillibeer's original Omnibus service, seems to have passed quite unnoticed in this connection, although in reality it marked the beginning of a new era in the history of the London bus. By allocating chassis 661008 to the East Surrey Traction Co, the LGOC avoided offering any hostages to the Public Carriage Office when it had other ideas on the type of body it intended to use on the Regent chassis for its own services. At this time the bus was still owned by AEC; however, the LGOC bought it on 31 December following, whereupon it became one of those owned by the LGOC although operated by the East Surrey Traction Co. On purchase by the LGOC it received a body number (10954). It passed to London General Country Services in 1932 and in due course to the LPTB, in whose fleet in 1935 it received the number

Below:
ST1139, in its final form with half-drop windows and cab side partly filled and glazed, at Windsor in 1947. *Author*

23

ST1139. It survived with its original body little altered until 1948.

Another of these pre-production demonstrators with a similar Short Bros body, 661004, was allocated to Tilling. Tilling had previously bought its buses from its own Tilling-Stevens subsidiary and this AEC initiative apparently involved the good offices of the LGOC, as the bus in question was delivered to Chiswick on 10 July and licensed by the LGOC on behalf of Tilling on 12 July. Tilling chose not to buy this bus after its demonstration period and it thus disappeared from the Tilling London fleet before the formation of the LPTB. However, it left its mark on the London scene in a way which the LGOC-East Surrey demonstrator did not, as Tilling adopted the Regent in quite a big way for service both in London and Brighton and the bodies which it built for some 300 of these chassis over the next three years bore quite a perceptible resemblance to this Rackham-Short Bros demonstrator. The London allocation of 191 of these buses passed to the LPTB on 1 October 1933, receiving the numbers

ST837-1027, and are dealt with more fully in Chapter 7.

The first Renown chassis, 663001, which was to become LT1, was also built in the Experimental Department at AEC. Contractually it was the first chassis of a batch of 50 buses numbered LT1-50 which were to be covered by LGOC sanction No 24/977. At this stage it is doubtful if a formal order had been placed for these chassis but they were covered by the notice of intent which the LGOC had given AEC and 50 body numbere (10278-10327) had been allocated for the bodies for them. These were in the batch of 250 which had been reserved before the 16 experimental buses detailed in Chapter 1 were sanctioned. However, the chassis of LT1 was delivered to Chiswick on 24 June practically six months before LT2-50. LT1 was licensed on 2 August 1929 with a body numbered 10185 and not one of the bodies from the reserved batch.

The body 10185, whose number falls between the bodies built for NS2372-2377 and those for 14 Reliances built in June for the services operated by the National company, was originally put in hand in connection with a plan to shorten one of the LS-type buses to 27ft (something that actually happened when four of these vehicles were converted to breakdown lorries after withdrawal). According to the contemporary body stock book this body was actually taken into stock at the end of April, but the plan to shorten an LS was abandoned when AEC offered to build the model 663 Renown. The LS-type which was built on a wheelbase of 18ft 6in and was 29ft long (18ft 10½in and 29ft 11in in the case of LS6) were restricted to certain routes by the Public Carriage Office and it seems likely that this is where the idea that 27ft would be an acceptable length for a three-axle double-decker may have originated. The City Omnibus Co's Leyland Titanics of 1933 conformed to this standard and even at this late date deferred to the Public Carriage Office's preference for outside staircases.

Naturally a body built for an LS chassis with its central differentials required fairly extensive rework to exploit the potential of the Renown, with its offset differentials, for a significantly lower floor level. This rework would have involved not only the main pillars but the platform and staircase as well as the cab structure. This work no doubt occupied much of the period which elapsed between arrival of the chassis at Chiswick on 24 June and its entry into service licensed on 2 August.

This body was of outside staircase design having six bays between lower deck bulkheads at 36in pillar spacing. The upper saloon extended for another half bay forward over the cab and a similar amount rearward over the platform. The roof overhung the upper deck front windows of which two, set at an angle, spanned the width of the body instead of the four used in previous double-deck bodies. Similarly the cab canopy overhung the cab, which was a prominent feature of the body with a square front and sloping glass windscreen. Although the cab had no door, it was carried on the body together with the offside front wing; this last was supplied by the chassis manufacturer, as was the cab floor, side and dash panels. With these exceptions the body was panelled entirely in aluminium. Chiswick works was already a leader in the techniques of producing shaped panels in this material. All the foregoing description applies also to the 49 bodies built for LT2-50 six months later.

The glass windscreen was one of three significant innovations pioneered with the body of LT1. Nowadays when a windscreen is something which every driver takes for granted it is hard to realise that it could ever have been an innovation, but it was in a London bus in 1929. Only in May that year the Public Carriage Office gave the LGOC approval for windscreens to be fitted to 100 buses for operation on Stage Carriage services within the Metropolitan Police District. The LGOC managed in fact to get away with 101 (LT1-50, ST1 and the first 50 T-type bodies) — before the Public Carriage Office insisted on subsequent buses being built without windscreens for the next 12 months.

The second new feature making its first appearance in a London bus was the use all round of internally illuminated roller blind destination boxes. These had already been used in the bodies for the 14 Reliances for the National services built at Chiswick in June, in which they were fitted at the front only, and in the tunnel NS bodies, in which they were used at the rear only. In the body of LT1 a box of the size used in the Reliances was fitted front and rear. The use of a box limited to the height of the roof of a single-decker severely restricted the amount of route information conveyed to prospective passengers compared with the board displays used on the NS and LS-types. This shortcoming was apparently quickly recognised in the case of single-deckers because in all subsequent full-size single-deck bodies, including those for T1-50 built in the closing months of 1929, the destination boxes were made wider. Double-deck buses however continued to be turned out with boxes of the size used in LT1 until November 1931, after which new bodies were given a comprehensive three-blind display and earlier bodies were fitted on overhaul with a deeper front box which protruded from the panelling. On the outside-stair bodies fitted to LT1-50 the rear box did not lend itself to enlargement; it was accordingly devoted to destination and route information, and the route number was transferred to a stencil.

The third new feature introduced on LT1 was the use of half-drop windows. These can be clearly seen in London Transport pictures of LT1 taken during its first few days of service in August 1929. In this body the radius at the top corners was attached to the opening portion, creating a rather unusual effect when the window was open. In all subsequent double-deck bus bodies of Chiswick design built up until the end of 1931 radii at the tops of the windows were formed on the fixed metal louvres instead of the window itself.

This brings us to the special features which distinguished the body of LT1 from those built for LT2-50. These included seats which although filled with curled hair were of a different design and only 54 in number (24 downstairs, 30 upstairs) compared with 60 (28/32) which were packed into the bodies built for LT2-50. The latter were of the square-backed design used in Chiswick bodies throughout 1930. In a press statement in 1929 the LGOC had expressed the opinion that 54 was about the optimum number of seats for buses in London service; however, I have often wondered if some relaxation such as an increase in the permitted gross weight may have been allowed in vehicles of this category first registered after 1 January 1930, as LT1 carried its original body for its whole life until it was scrapped in 1948 and its seating capacity was never increased. I have no reason to doubt that one of the spare bodies built for LT2-150 could have been fitted had this been allowed.

As first built LT1 had no moulding below the upper deck windows; although there was one below the lower deck windows this was shallower than the later standard. Raised waistrail mouldings of the sizes which were so characteristic of the LT, ST and T-type bodies were added to the body of LT1 in the course of an overhaul during the war, when it also acquired a cab of the later round-fronted pattern. The windows had earlier been changed to the standard type. However this body had two features it was to retain throughout its life which belong architecturally with LS-type rather than the LT-type. These were skirt panels with reverse curvature and the shape of the front upper deck panelling, which was flat across the front with a curve at each side — the shape used in the NS and LS-type bodies with board displays and corner windows. In all later LT and ST bodies the panelling was bevelled from the pillar to the destination box. These details added to the interest of seeing LT1 in traffic towards the end of its life, which extended for more than 10 years after the NS and LS-types had disappeared from the London scene.

Undoubtedly an outside staircase was something which the LGOC would have preferred not to have in the LT-type. Its use in the body which was diverted to LT1 was a legacy of the bruising which the company had received from the Public Carriage Office over the LS-type and a consequent policy of keeping its powder dry for the submission of the new inside-staircase design with ST1, features of which it was also desired to use in the CC-type. There would in fact have been time to alter the design of the LT-type body between the approval of ST1 in October 1929 and the building of LT2-50 in January and February 1930. The reason that this opportunity was not taken may have been that the belief that the future lay with the Chiswick chassis (approved in the same sanction as ST1) was then at its peak of credibility, in which case the LT-type may have been seen as simply a stopgap until the Chiswick chassis began rolling off the production line.

When first built LT1 did not have brakes on the front wheels. This is something which only came to light a few years ago, when Alan Townsin published a selection of AEC works photographs in *Blue Triangle* and when it did, it was quite unexpected. The thinking revealed betrays an inability to move forward from the LS-type — and this was much more likely to have been on the part of somebody at Chiswick than of

Below:
LT1 in Regent Street in April 1930. Although it is still working from Cricklewood the waistrail moulding and upper deck panelling, originally white, are now painted red, indicating a visit to Chiswick when front brakes were probably also fitted.
LT 22915

Rackham. The works photograph of the newly completed chassis probably shows it in the form in which it was delivered to Chiswick and this is how LT1 would have entered service in August 1929. Almost certainly front brakes and the two chassis-mounted slave cylinders to operate them would have been added within the next few months, very likely before delivery of the chassis of LT2-50 commenced in December or January. The licensing weight for LT1 was 7T14C; this corresponds to a figure some 4cwt heavier later in the 1930s when the formula had been changed to one with fuel tanks full instead of practically empty. This is something which needs to be borne in mind when considering the licensing weights of other vehicles mentioned in this book.

When LT1 was licensed at the beginning of August 1929 it was put to work from Cricklewood on Route 16. The accompanying photograph shows it still working from Cricklewood in March 1930, but I have another showing it working from Plumstead in 1935 when it was still in its original condition except for the windows and the front destination box. During and after the 1939-45 war it was at Leyton, together with many of its outside-stair sisters which were still to be seen daily in Central London working on routes 10, 35, 38 and 38A.

The next new bus to be completed at Chiswick was ST1, licensed on 31 October 1929. The cancellation of the two long-wheelbase Renowns left ST1 as the only complete bus on an AEC chassis covered by sanction 24/918, although this still included a Regent instruction chassis. The chassis of ST1 as delivered, 661074, seems to have been a perfectly standard Regent with offside fuel tank. However, the body, 10493, was a complete departure from anything seen in London before. Its most innovative feature was a full-width enclosed loading platform from which a straight staircase ascended forwards over the offside wheel arch. As first built it had seats for 50 passengers, 20 downstairs and 30 up. The seats differed slightly from later ST bodies which seated only 49 (20/29) and the weight for licensing was 6 tons 6 cwt; with all seats occupied at 16 passengers to the ton it was therefore up to the gross weight limit for two-axle buses, at that time 9½ tons. The seats were arranged with four transverse rows downstairs and four longitudinal seats over the nearside wheel arch; upstairs, there was a seat for five across the rear behind the staircase well, then three triple seats (the foremost one of which was later reduced to a double in conformity with later bodies) and then four transverse rows (in pairs). The front end treatment of the bus was generally similar to LT1, with the top deck carried only half way forward over the cab and the roof and cab canopy both overhanging. The cab although differing in detail was similar to that used for LT1, square fronted with a sloping windscreen. There was, however, a difference in the treatment of the front upper deck panelling, which was bevelled instead of rounded at the sides of the destination box. All the opening windows were of the later half-drop type and there were raised waistrail mouldings on both decks. The body was described as being of the Pullman type in some contemporary LGOC documents and certainly the whole effect was of a very civilised bus compared with the NS-type.

The design of ST1 was made available to Ransomes Sims & Jefferies of Ipswich which built 60 bodies on AEC Regent chassis in the spring of 1930, 42 for the ESTC and 18 for Autocar. The 42 built for the ESTC replaced the same number of K-types operated by that company, 30 of which were LGOC-owned, and consequently 30 of the new buses were LGOC-owned and had

Right:
T38, the first purpose-built Green Line coach, at Golders Green in 1936. *J. F. Higham*

LGOC body numbers (11105-11134) from the start. Six of the remaining 12 were transferred from ESTC to LGOC ownership in August, receiving body numbers 11537-11542. All these buses passed in due course to London Transport, receiving the bonnet numbers ST1091-1132 when the country buses were numbered in 1935. Four of the Autocar buses for which the company had been unsuccessful in obtaining licences were transferred to the East Surrey the following November, when they were the subject of an LGOC sanction (24/1056) and received LGOC body numbers (12355-8). These passed to London Transport in due course becoming ST1085-1088. Unlike ST1 these buses retained their offside fuel tanks and small destination boxes throughout their lives, which extended until 1948-49. One, ST1108, was even painted red and transferred to Dalston for the last few months of its life.

Although it was licensed on 31 October 1929 ST1 did not enter service until 1 March 1930 when it was sent to Hanwell with a large batch of later buses beginning with ST3. It seems likely that in the intervening four months the fuel tank was moved to the nearside in conformity with all the subsequent ST-type buses built for the LGOC and its subsidiaries but that the body still had its square-fronted cab with windscreen. Certainly when coded in 1934 ST1 was included in chassis code 1ST (the only other chassis code raised for ex-LGOC vehicles) in Central Area stock being 1/1ST for any which still only had one servo). However, the body code ST1 was only applied to the body 10493, and this was linked to a square-fronted cab in a document from which I made a note at Chiswick in 1946. All the Chiswick-design bodies built during 1930 which came into Central Area stock were coded ST1/1. At some time later the

body 10493 received a round-fronted cab in the course of overhaul. I saw it once, in about 1946 when it was on ST248, and the only distinguishing detail I could then detect was that the black band between the decks was convex instead of flat, as it also was in the Ransomes bodies on the Country Area buses.

The next buses to appear from Chiswick, in November and December 1929, were single-deckers numbered T1-50 on AEC Regal chassis with offside fuel tanks. These had originally been included in the notice of intent to AEC and had since been covered by the LGOC sanction 24/953, with body numbers 10228-10277. They were of straightforward six-bay design with an open rear platform and seated 29. The 26ft long bodies were very similar in design to the 14 built for the National Reliances the previous June, but had waistrail mouldings, half-drop windows and wider destination boxes. The cabs were similar to that described for ST1.

There were two exceptions. The first was T38, which was requisitioned as a chassis to serve as the basis for what was to become the first Green Line coach. For this purpose it was given a body which was much plainer and more bus-like than previous LGOC coaches — these had been intended for private hire and tours — with a fixed roof and half-drop windows. Although it employed the same six-bay construction as the buses, the floor in this body was made appreciably higher so that all the seats, of which there were 28, could face forward. There were two internal steps from a swing door behind the rear wheel. A central rear emergency door was also provided; this door was glazed but the panels at either side were not. At the front the cab was round-fronted and the roof canopy was given a much more rounded shape and

Left:
T43 when new with eight-cylinder engine. Note the bonnet extension and also the short bay over the rear wheels, a feature of this body which survived both its subsequent transfer to T10 and later conversion to front entrance. *W. Noel Jackson*

included a single-line destination blind. Above this an illuminated sign was later added. Upon completion in March 1930, T38 was put to work on the original Golders Green-Watford route started the previous December together with nine of the 14 National Reliances which exchanged bodies with ADC 416s for this purpose. T38 spent its whole life on this duty until withdrawal in 1939.

The other exception, T43, was if anything even more interesting. The chassis was received from AEC at the end of December fitted with an in-line eight-cylinder engine of 87mm bore and 130mm stroke. This was to be the first of five such engines numbered SE1-5 which were to be fitted in new AEC chassis delivered within the next couple of months; the others were fitted in LT35 and 41 and ST4 and 84.

To anyone who can remember the NS-type the thought that anybody in 1929 could have regarded the level of refinement achieved with the new AEC six-cylinder overhead camshaft engine as inadequate will give rise to astonishment. However, at this time straight-eight engines were appearing in some higher priced cars and there was someone at Chiswick — this may have been the Development Engineer, a man named Watson — who was interested in engine design. The rolling stock card of LS1 recorded that it was fitted with an LGOC twin-camshaft six-cylinder engine of 108mm bore and 140mm stroke from November 1928 until October 1929. Presumably this was a conversion of the AEC A121 engine, but it must have involved new castings and camshafts and even though it only ran for a short time this brief note on the card discloses the existence at Chiswick of considerable design ability.

The AEC eight-cylinder engine was never given any publicity, and so far as is known

the five engines for the LGOC were the only ones ever built. The inference is that they were produced to satisfy some particular interest existing within the LGOC. This was still the time when the LGOC's plan to design and build its own bus chassis at Chiswick was at the peak of its credibility, after the building of prototypes had been authorised and before the attendant problems had begun to become apparent. One of the most distinctive features of the first two Chiswick chassis, LT1000 and 1051, was an exceptionally long bonnet and in the five bodies which were completed to suit this design the bulkhead behind the engine was in a noticeably more rearward position than that which it occupied on AEC chassis. It seems likely that the CC-type was designed to take an eight-cylinder engine, and that these AEC eight-cylinder engines were produced as a bid to retain the LGOC business in the event of an engine of this type becoming a requirement.

In T43 and other chassis delivered with AEC eight-cylinder engines the bulkhead was in the standard position and the driver's structure and cab were completely standard. Naturally the engine was longer and this extra length was accommodated by moving the radiator forward some 6in and fitting an offside bonnet of this length between the radiator and the cab. In the case of T43 only, the body was shortened at the rear to compensate. This shortening took place in the bay over the wheel arch, so that the pillar behind this was hard up against the rear wing. This arrangement allowed the entrance and platform to be kept at the same width as the standard T-type bodies or almost so.

The AEC eight-cylinder engine was, I have been told, of the overhead camshaft type and doubtless the design of the timing case and many of the valve gear details were thus common to the standard six-cylinder engine. However, although the swept volume of the eight-cylinder engine was the same as that of the 100mm bore six-cylinder unit the rated power at 85bhp was 10bhp less. Almost certainly this reduction was due to the difficulties of obtaining satisfactory mixture distribution in an in-line eight-cylinder engine with a single carburettor — something which the car manufacturers offering models with engines of this type were also to discover.

The body fitted to T43, 10276, was the 49th of the batch and the last to be needed until the following July when T156, the replacement ordered for T38 on sanction No 24/1003, made its appearance. T43 was licensed in mid-January 1930 and sent to Holloway. It ran with the eight-cylinder engine until the following December when a standard six-cylinder engine was substituted on overhaul. Rather surprisingly T43 also then received a body of standard length and the shortened body was transferred to T10. T10 thereafter carried the shortened body until disposal in 1952, still with the short bay over the rear wheel arch which survived conversion to front entrance in 1934. As mentioned in Chapter 2, in the

coding given to these buses on conversion T10 received the code 1T1 whereas T43 was uniquely given the code 2T2, this being a nonsense.

T27 was converted on overhaul in December 1930 to a doorless front entrance layout with central rear emergency door. This conversion was undertaken to try out this layout which it was intended to use in the LT-type single-deckers, the first of which, LT1001, was licensed in January 1931. From this point onwards, all new single-deck buses and coaches over whose design Chiswick had any say, had front entrances and rear emergency doors. As we shall see shortly, this layout was also applied to coaches licensed from the beginning of 1931 onwards. However, some years were to elapse before the remaining T-type buses were converted. The LGOC body stock book at 30 June 1933 showed eight as having been converted by that date; all the remaining buses which by then belonged to the Central Area of London Transport were converted between March 1934 and January 1935 (at least this is so where the cards had dated entries). This category did not include T15, 21, 25, 26 and 35, which were allocated to Crayford and in April 1931 were

Below:
LT42, working from Nunhead, in Trafalgar Square, April 1930.
LT 23329

Left:
**LT91, with one of the bodies built
for the second batch of LT type
double-deckers, at Leytonstone in
1935.** *LT U16831*

transferred with that garage and its routes to the ESTC; these buses passed to LGCS the following year and then to London Transport's Country Area, where in 1935 they resumed their original numbers with the suffix B. They remained in their original rear-entrance condition until disposal in 1939.

Sixteen AEC Regals with bus bodies of the same Chiswick rear-entrance design were built by Hall Lewis & Co for the ESTC in March and April 1930. Six of these which were LGOC-owned had LGOC body numbers (11135-11140). These buses also passed via LGCS to London Transport, in whose fleet they received the numbers T372-379B and 383-390B in 1935. These also remained in their original condition until withdrawal in 1939; some of which were not disposed of immediately carried snow-ploughs during the war and at its conclusion were sold to the Allied Control Commission for use in Germany. Hall Lewis also built similar bodies on five Regals for Autocar at the same time as the East Surrey vehicles; these passed to Maidstone and District on the formation of London Transport.

The Central Area T-type buses had an exceptionally long life in London Transport service. As well as worm and nut steering boxes, the D124 gearbox modification and 20in wheels they all received brake conversion in 1931. In 1950 they were given 7.7-litre diesel engines from scrapped STL-type buses at least five years their junior. They lasted in London Transport service until 1952, mainly on outer suburban services worked from Kingston and some other garages.

Having completed the 50 T-type bus bodies, Chiswick returned to the 50 LT-type double-deckers included in the notice of intent which had been given to AEC. These had now been covered by a formal LGOC sanction, No 24/977. LT2-50 were licensed in January and February 1930. The 49 bodies built for these 49 chassis were given the numbers 10278-10326, in the batch which has been reserved for the buses covered by the notice of intent. The 50th body was never built; as we have seen, LT1 had been completed as a preproduction prototype with a body which was the subject of an earlier authorisation and the sanction did not provide for a spare.

The bodies built for LT2-50 conformed with the body of LT1 in all major respects; they had outside staircases and the same six-bay construction between lower saloon bulkheads with 36in pillar spacing. However, the seating was increased to 60 (28 down, 32 up). The seats themselves were of the square-backed type as used in all other Chiswick bus bodies until the end of 1930. The raised waistrail mouldings on both decks which were to be characteristic of all subsequent Chiswick bodies for the ST, LT and T-types were now incorporated; the half-drop windows and their surrounds were likewise of standard type and the front upper deck panelling was bevelled from the destination box. The lower deck panelling had a prominent wooden moulding; the skirt panels only curved in at the bottom and did not have the reverse curvature used in LT1. These bodies all originally had square-fronted cabs with windscreens; the design of these was identical with those of the T-type bodies and differed slightly from the original cab of the body fitted to LT1.

The chassis all had front brakes as delivered. The licensing weight of these

buses was given, in their later years at least, as 7ton 18cwt. LT35 and 41 were delivered from AEC with eight-cylinder engines, serial Nos SE2 and 3, as described above in connection with T43, which they carried until their first overhaul 12 months later. When new, these buses were allocated to Nunhead and Plumstead.

A further 100 similar buses, LT51-150, were ordered later in 1930 on sanction 24/1011 and placed in traffic in July and August. The bodies built against this sanction, 11169-11268, differed from the earlier bodies in having round-fronted cabs without windscreens. Five spares, 12005-12009, were built before the end of the year so that they were available by the time LT2-50 came in for their first overhaul. Thenceforth bodies with the round-fronted and square-fronted cabs were spread haphazardly over the whole of LT2-150; during the war some of the earlier bodies were also rebuilt with the later type of cab.

Quite extensive alterations were made to LT1-150 during 1931. As well as the fitting of windscreens to all the bodies which originally did not have them, the chassis specification was altered on overhaul to the 110mm bore engine with which which the axle ratio was changed to 6.75 : 1; AEC worm and nut steering boxes were fitted in place of the Marles units (it is possible that LT51-150 may have had worm and nut steering from new) and the constant mesh conversion for third gear was incorporated in the gearbox. After this the whole group with two exceptions remained substantially unaltered for the rest of their lives. The front destination boxes were enlarged in 1932, when a stencil for the rear route number was also added; this was removed during the war. These buses were then due for replacement but the war dictated their retention and throughout it (and for a couple of years afterwards) they were a familiar sight in Central London working from Leyton, Loughton and Potters Bar. When these garages received an allocation of the Leyland PD1 Titans in 1946 some of the outside-stair LTs were dispersed to other garages for use as rush-hour reliefs. However, as late as 1947 one could still ride up Whitehall or Shaftesbury Avenue in a petrol-engined three-axle bus with outside stairs, a vintage experience such as one could not have enjoyed in any other town in Britain for many years.

The most important exception made among the buses of this batch was LT21, which was fitted in June 1935 with an AEC 7.7-litre Comet Mk 1 oil engine. It was then sent to Mortlake, still with its outside-stair body. In March 1940 LT21 was given an inside-stair body, the code being changed from 2/2LT2/2 to 2/12LT3/4. With the conversion of all the A165 8.8-litre engines to direct injection, Mortlake by 1943 housed all the remaining LT-type buses still having AEC-Ricardo oil engines (the 32 buses of code 4LT, which we shall come to later). LT21, which still retained its 6.75 : 1 axle ratio, was quite a lively performer. In 1946 when I got a chance to look inside the bonnet the engine was still of the Comet Mk 1 type. LT21 was the only conversion ever undertaken by London Transport using the A171 engine and it was the only bus of the outside-stair group ever converted to diesel. It lasted until 1948.

The only other exception was LT26, which was fitted at the end of 1945 with an inside-staircase body of the later 1931 type. Coded 1/2LT5/8, it was then allocated to Plumstead. In this case the original petrol engine was retained and as the last of the buses of code 2LT had been converted to diesel in 1940, LT26 was for the rest of its life the only petrol-engined example of the LT-type with an inside staircase body and a crash gearbox.

Delivery of ST-type buses to garages, licensed and ready for service, began in March 1930. Over the remaining 10 months of 1930 500 ST-type buses were placed in LGOC service and a further 15 were completed for the services in the Watford area operated by the National Omnibus & Transport Co. As we have seen, the notice of intent given to AEC included the latter 15 plus 100 of the former, whereas the sanction 24/918 clearly envisaged the construction of 515 buses between the prototype ST1 and the instruction chassis for the Training School, which was to be ST517.

The first LGOC sanction raised, 24/979, covered 300 vehicles, ST2-301, plus nine spare bodies (body numbers 10377-10476, 10503-10702, 10955-10963). The chassis differed from ST1 as first delivered in having nearside fuel tanks; also ST4 and 84 were delivered with eight-cylinder engines, serial numbers SE4 and 5, which they carried until first overhaul 12 months later. The bodies as built differed from ST1 in having only 49 seats (20 downstairs, 29 up) and round-fronted cabs without windscreens. ST2 although delivered from AEC in November 1929 was used as a mobile instruction chassis until June 1931, when it was the last standard ST-type bus to be licensed. Over the intervening 16 months the ST-type buses replaced those of the K-type which until then were still a mainstay of the General fleet. This programme involved building, with spares, 884 bodies of standard LGOC design, an average of 55 a month. To leave some capacity at Chiswick for bodies of other types during this period, 130 of these bodies were contracted out to Shorts and Strachans in addition to six special bodies built by Shorts and one by Metro-Cammell.

ST502-516 were ordered against LGOC Sanction 24/995, with body numbers 11149-11163. These were the chassis originally intended for the National services and

Left:
ST 140, one of the six buses with Short Bros six-bay lowbridge bodies with two upper gangways built for the Watford services in 1930, at Watford circa 1935.
J. F. Higham

Right:
ST150, with the prototype Metro-Cammell all-metal body built in 1930, seen in Park Lane in 1947. *Author*

Below:
T151 (originally numbered T153) one of the LGOC private hire coaches of 1930, in December 1934, with LGCS bonnet number plate. *LT 22777*

included in the notice of intent to AEC. They had chassis numbers 661783-797 which although later than ST2-301 (661148 and 211-509, less 362, which was diverted to an independent) were earlier than ST302-501 (661800-999). Chassis 661798 was ST517, and 661799 replaced 661362 as ST154.

In the event, although the 15 chassis for the National Services and the one for Chiswick Training School were treated as a related group, the chassis actually used for the National Services were ST107, 111, 116, 129, 132, 135, 136, 140, 141, 143, 152, 157, 159, 162 and 163, and ST169 became the instruction chassis. It was still in the Training School when I was at Chiswick in 1946.

The National services in the Watford area included a route between Watford and Chesham, worked jointly with Amersham & District, which required lowbridge vehicles. To cater for this requirement ST136, 140, 141, 157, 162 and 163 were sent to Short Bros to be fitted with lowbridge bodies. These bodies, originally numbered 11158-11163, were of that company's design and had nothing in common with any standard Chiswick body although this fact became disguised in the course of later overhauls when they were given Chiswick top-dressing in the form of such things as waistrail mouldings. This process was still continuing after the war. The body itself was a six-bay inside-stair design with a corner staircase and two side gangways on the top deck, where there were eight triple seats. There were also 24 seats in the lower saloon. These buses are interesting for having been the last examples of the ST-type to survive; in 1950 they were converted to diesel with 7.7-litre engines

from scrapped STLs and they lasted until 1952. The other nine vehicles sent to Watford had standard Chiswick bodies, initially without windscreens even though they were based outside the Metropolitan Police district. All these buses passed to LGCS in 1932, to Country Area on the formation of the LPTB and resumed their original bonnet numbers with the suffix B in 1935.

ST302-501, which followed after ST502-516 and 154 between September and December 1930, were covered by LGOC Sanction 24/1010. These chassis probably all had AEC worm and nut steering boxes from new and very likely triple servo brakes as well, whereas the earlier vehicles only acquired this equipment on later overhaul. An interesting vehicle licensed in October was ST211, which was fitted with a Metro-Cammell metal-framed body (11535, following the 200 standard bodies, 11335-11534, included in the sanction for ST302-501). Although the design of this body followed that of the standard Chiswick product fairly closely, it was distinguishable at a glance; it obviously had good lasting qualities, surviving until 1949, latterly on ST150. It apparently made a good impression on the LGOC, as similar, though longer, bodies (13030-13054) were ordered for 25 Dennis Lances bought the following year for the Overground services on sanction 24/1084. Of still greater import-ance, however, were ST462, 464 and 466, which were fitted when new with AEC-Acro oil engines; after taking part in a demon-stration at AEC in December these three buses entered service at Willesden at the end of the year. The advent of the diesel engine is covered in detail in Chapter 5; all

Above:
The much-travelled T369 at Harefield in January 1935.
LT U16670

that needs to be said here is that after running in the ST-type buses for a year the diesel engines were removed at their first overhaul. After rework the engines were transferred to LT-type buses early in 1932 and ST462, 464 and 466 emerged from overhaul as standard examples of their type.

All the other vehicles on AEC chassis licensed by the LGOC in 1930 were coaches. These included five Regals, T150-4, which were covered by the notice of intent; they were intended for private hire use and for this purpose they were sent to Hoyals, a

coachbuilder in Weybridge, to be fitted with 32-seat coach bodies having folding roofs and swing doors. The chassis were early standard production Regals with offside fuel tanks. Not being intended for stage carriage use T150-4 were 27ft long. They were licensed in May, although according to my notes they were included in sanction 24/1011 with LT51-150 which did not appear until the summer, and allocated to the LGOC's coach depot in Brixton. After the formation of Green Line Coaches Ltd in July the private hire function was transferred to the Green Line which in turn was transferred to LGCS on 29 July 1932. T150-4 thus became part of the LPTB Country Area fleet. They originally had body Nos 8856-60 in the special series reserved for charabancs and service vehicles, but these were allowed to lapse in LGCS days. A most curious thing, noted earlier, is that LGCS reversed the bonnet numbers to make these run in sequence with the registration numbers whereas they had originally been in the reverse order. T150-4 were sold in 1938, after the arrival of the LTC-type coaches.

New coaches were also needed in 1930 for the introduction of the Green Line services. Although the AEC Regal chassis was a natural first choice, the layout of the body built on the appropriated T38 was clearly not ideal. Sanction 24/996 covered 100 chassis with nearside fuel tanks; these were T51-149 and 155, this last actually being the first chassis delivered. A completely new body design was produced, having seven bays instead of six. Of these the foremost, which on the offside was occupied by the emergency door, was shorter than the remainder, whereas the rearmost, which was occupied by the entrance, was longer on the nearside only. Because it was not possible to accommodate an entrance of acceptable width on the rear overhang with a sliding door within an overall length of 26ft the solution adopted was to recess a swing door into the body. This arrangement reduced the seating capacity to 27, all facing forward.

T155 and 51-149 were licensed in May, June and July; of the 100 bodies (11004-11103), 50 were built at Chiswick and 25 each by Hall Lewis and Shorts. Fifty further coaches of the same design were built in September and October against Sanction 24/1025; the bodies for these (11285-11334) were built 25 each by Hall Lewis and Shorts. These chassis had triple servo brakes and worm and nut steering from new. These coaches lasted until 1938, when they were replaced by new 30-seat coaches of the 10T10-type. In the next and all subsequent deliveries of coaches for the Green Line services a front sliding door layout was adopted. The rear entrance coaches were mostly disposed of in 1938-39 but some which were still in stock at the outbreak of war were kept in reserve until its end, when they were sold to the Allied Control Commission. A solitary exception, T120, which was made into an ambulance during the war, was converted in 1946 to 1/7T7/1 specification with a front entrance body from T305 and survived in bus service until 1949.

Although this brings us to an end of AEC buses and coaches built by the LGOC for its own services in 1930, an interesting vehicle bodied at Chiswick in October may perhaps be mentioned. This was an AEC Regal built for demonstration in Lima, Peru, for which purpose it was completed with a body numbered 11536 closely derived from the T-type bus body, but with a round-fronted cab (which had a door), full-drop windows and an open rear platform on the right-hand side. By an irony of fate this vehicle returned to Britain and came into the London Transport fleet, and will be described in a later chapter. This body is believed to have been the last rear entrance single-deck body built by the LGOC.

Below:
Leatherhead ESTC garage in October 1930, showing two of the 42 AEC Regent double-deckers built for the ESTC with Ransomes bodies to the design of ST1, one of the 16 AEC Regal single-deckers with Hall Lewis bodies built to the LGOC T-type design, with a single-deck K-type and two PS-type buses. This is obviously a posed photograph, the Regal being fitted with a coach blind for the occasion.
LT U7413

4: The Chiswick Chassis

Of the 12 buses on chassis to be built at Chiswick authorised on sanction 24/918, only two of the CC-type were completed in 1930. Surprisingly, these were numbered in the LT series. The first, numbered LT1000, was completed in July with body 10478 and having been licensed on the 31st was sent to Nunhead for service. The second, numbered LT1051, was completed in September with body 10479. The intervening numbers LT1001-1050 had meanwhile been allocated to the first 50 LT single-deckers. LT1051 was not licensed until 12 months later, being presumably retained at Chiswick meanwhile for development work. Three further bodies, 10480/1/2, were also completed in September 1930. From this we can deduce that the decision to prune the sanction from six to four CC-type and from six to three CB-type cannot have been taken until these bodies were already in hand. As we shall see, these last three bodies were later adapted for use on AEC LT-type chassis.

These bodies resembled ST1 in having a large loading platform and a straight inside staircase extending forward from it on the offside. As fitted to the CC-type chassis they seated 54 but the three which were later fitted to AEC chassis seated 56. The platform appears in fact to have been identical with the ST type, with a pillar spacing of the rearmost bay of 38½in, whereas the pillar spacing of the six bays between the lower deck bulkheads was only about 35¼in. This was because the front bulkhead behind the engine was some 3in further aft than the position it occupied on AEC chassis. This was to allow room for a bonnet fully 5ft long, the nearside panel of which was in two pieces. There was also a detachable panel on the offside in front of the cab, which rode on the chassis completely separate from the body. As first built

Below:
LT1000 as first built, at Chiswick in July 1930. Note that the cab is separate from the body and although at this stage it has no windscreen, it has a small door.
Author's Collection

there was no windscreen, but the cab was provided with a low, waist-high door.

Within the bonnet there was a six-cylinder overhead valve petrol engine of 100mm bore and 130mm stroke. This was obtained from Henry Meadows & Sons of Wolverhampton, an independent firm of engine manufacturers which built engines for Lagonda Cars about that time and possibly others. Circumstantial evidence suggests that the purpose of the long bonnet was to accommodate a straight-eight engine, but no such engine was ever fitted to either LT1000 or 1051. The radiator fitted to these and the subsequent Chiswick chassis was not a thing of beauty, with the sides tapering inwards from bottom to top and the name GENERAL cast into the top tank.

The engine drove through a single-plate clutch to a separately mounted four-speed gearbox, the control for which was mounted on the engine. The drive continued to a rear bogie with fully floating shafts — the only feature which could be said to be more advanced than the equivalent in contemporary AEC chassis. This was probably supplied complete by Kirkstall Forge. Certainly the hub caps resembled those found on Guy trolleybuses and other known users of Kirkstall axles. The front axle was likewise also probably a Kirkstall product and a Marles steering box completed the specification. The axle ratio used was 8.33:1 and the licensing weight 8ton 4cwt.

A prominent and distinctive feature of the five original bodies built for the CC-type in 1930 was that the cab canopy and the overhang of the top deck were lengthened to compensate for the more rearward position of the bulkhead. The three bodies (10480-10482) which were adapted for use on AEC chassis in March 1931 were provided with an extended version of the standard round-fronted cab with windscreen and also a make-up piece to bridge the gap between the bulkhead and the rear of the standard AEC bonnet.

In February 1931 the bodies were removed from both LT1000 and LT1051 while various modifications were made to the chassis. These included moving the gearbox to a new position 9¼in further aft. When the bodies were refitted at the end of April they were put back in the reverse order, 10479 now being on LT1000, 10478 on LT1051. By this time these buses would have been fitted with windscreens; as the cab was mounted separately from the body the arrangement must have resembled that which can be seen in the illustration of T1000 on the next page.

Below:
Another view of LT1000 showing the two-piece bonnet.
Author's Collection

T1000, the first of the CB-type, was the next of the chassis to be completed, on 20 May 1931. In this vehicle the bulkhead was in the normal position relative to the front wheels which it occupied on AEC chassis; clearly there was no idea of fitting an eight-cylinder engine in a four-wheeled single-decker. However, the bonnet side panel was still in two pieces and there was still a detachable panel in front of the cab scuttle on the offside. As built T1000 also had a six-cylinder Meadows engine of 100mm bore and 130mm stroke but in this case the separately mounted gearbox only had three speeds (with central control). A Marles steering box and Kirkstall axles were again used, the rear axle being a fully floating design with a ratio of 7.67:1. The body, 10484, was a shortened version of the contemporary single-deck LT-type body with 30 seats of the square-backed type and only a front destination box. However, the cab was mounted separately on the chassis, in the manner used on the ADC416-type, although with windscreen. T1000 was placed in service at Kingston at the beginning of July.

The last four buses of the pruned sanction for Chiswick chassis were turned out in the autumn of 1931. In all four of these the more modern arrangement of cantilevering the cab from the body, as used on contempor-ary AEC chassis, was adopted, although the bonnet had the nearside panel still in two pieces and a detachable offside panel. They were probably also built with AEC worm and nut steering boxes. In other respects they shared the mechanical specification of the earlier examples of their respective types. LT1202 and 1203 were completed in September and October, being fitted with LT5-type bodies (12599 and 12600) from the series then in production for LT501-950, although having only 54 seats. They joined LT1000 and 1051 at Nunhead. T1001 and 1002 were completed in November and December. The bodies fitted to these two chassis (10485/6) resembled the later LT-type single-deckers, with front and rear destination boxes and 30 round-backed seats, and these two buses joined T1000 at Kingston.

It is hard to escape the impression that the LGOC management had lost interest in the Chiswick chassis by this time. The success of the AEC Regent, Regal and Renown, of which more than 2,000 had been ordered, was by now proved beyond doubt. Being lighter, they were better performers than the equivalent Chiswick chassis; what interest there had been in eight-cylinder petrol engines had come and gone (being satisfied, incidentally, by AEC and not by the Chiswick chassis) and more importantly,

Far left:
LT259 at Park Royal in 1947 with one of the bodies originally built for the CC-type. This was the only one of these bodies remaining in service after the war. *Author*

Below left:
T1000 working from Kingston in London Transport days. Note that the cab, although fitted with a windscreen, is mounted separately from the body. This was probably the arrangement applied to LT1000 and 1051 in April 1931. *J. F. Higham*

Below:
T1001 working from Kingston in 1932. This bus has the later arrangement of cab carried on the body, as also had T1002, LT1202 and 1203. Note that the bonnet is still in two pieces. *J. F. Higham*

Right:
LT1203, now fitted with AEC engine, gearbox and differential units, working from Streatham during its last year in service.
J. Bonell

new and promising types of both engine and transmission were now available from AEC as production options.

The next development involving one of the Chiswick chassis was in February 1932, when a Gardner 5LW five-cylinder diesel engine was fitted in LT1051. As recounted in the next chapter, it was a bad mistake when the development engineer in charge of the project advised the LGOC's chief engineer that the 5ft long bonnet of LT1051 would not accommodate a 6LW engine. However, it was a still worse mistake when with an engine giving only 85bhp at a governed speed of only 1,700rpm the bus was placed in service with an axle ratio of 7.67:1, which limited its top speed to 25mph: in postwar years Manchester successfully operated a whole fleet of 8ft wide Daimler buses, the weight of which can have been little less than that of LT1051, with Gardner 5LW engines, using an axle ratio of 6.2:1. Although this experiment was doomed to failure, LT1051 was sent to Harrow Weald to join the 32 buses with 130bhp AEC-Ricardo engines and with them was moved to Hanwell in April before it was abandoned in May.

LT1051 was next fitted with an AEC 110mm bore petrol engine and thus equipped returned to Nunhead in September. Its three sister CC-type buses were fitted with AEC petrol engines in 1933, that in LT1000 being of 100mm bore. At this stage the original 8.33:1 axle ratio was retained in these buses but in 1938 they were all given 110mm bore engines, AEC clutches and gearboxes and the rear axles were altered to accept AEC differential units of 6.75:1 ratio; LT1000 was thus treated in January, LT1202 in April, LT1051 in May, LT1203 in June. After this they were moved to Streatham from where they worked until withdrawal prior to sale in August 1939.

T1000, 1001 and 1002 were also given AEC 100mm bore 6-type petrol engines between December 1932 and November 1933, the axle ratio being changed at the same time to 6.5:1. The axles of these buses were also later altered to accept AEC differential units of 6.25:1 ratio, although the separate three-speed gearbox was retained. All three buses worked at Kingston until withdrawal in February 1938. After storage successively at Bromley, Chiswick Tram Depot and Bull Yard they were sold in August 1940, thereby escaping the air raid on Bull Yard in October.

Looked at from a distance of nearly 60 years, the whole story of the Chiswick chassis has an appearance of complete futility. After the fiasco of LT1051 the Development Department at Chiswick was closed and the engineer in charge of the project discharged. Had the buses not been numbered in the LT and T-types they might well have been withdrawn sooner than they were. On the other hand, once their final modifications had been made the four CC-type chassis with their shorter wheelbase might have made a better choice for conversion to recovery vehicles than the four examples of the LS-type which were chosen.

5: Diesel Engines, Fluid Transmission and Hydraulic Brakes, 1930-32

The AEC-Acro engine, type A155, fitted to ST462, 464 and 466 was the first diesel engine offered commercially on the British bus market. It was first shown to bus operators at a demonstration held at the AEC works at Southall in 1930. Throughout the 1930s the new type of power unit was invariably known in Britain as an oil engine, not a bad term perhaps when the most important distinction which most people who came into contact with buses — then still predominantly petrol-engined — had to make was to ensure that they were filled with the right fuel.

The attraction of the compression-ignition engine, to give it its formal name, was its much higher efficiency. The cycle efficiency of an internal combustion engine depends on its compression ratio; this is limited in a petrol engine, which breathes its fuel and air as a mixture, by the temperature rise on the compression stroke which must not be such as to create a risk of the compressed mixture detonating spontaneously. A diesel engine on the other hand only breathes air, and the compression temperature must be high enough to ignite the fuel when it is injected. The AEC-Acro engine had a

Below:
DST2, one of the three Daimler CH6 buses bought by the LGOC to try the Wilson gearbox/fluid flywheel transmission, working from Harrow Weald on Route 18 at Ludgate Circus, February 1931. *LT U8484*

compression ratio of 19:1 compared with 5.5:1 used in the contemporary AEC overhead camshaft petrol engine.

This theoretical advantage had been known for a long time. However, there was a daunting obstacle facing any vehicle manufacturer contemplating building an engine of this type in the fuel injection equipment, which required standards of hardness, precision and surface finish unknown in any part of a petrol engine. A ready-made solution to this problem became available in the late 1920s when the German firm Robert Bosch AG of Stuttgart introduced a new range of fuel injection equipment of high quality in sizes suitable for road vehicle engines.

Soon after his own appointment as Chief Engineer at AEC, Rackham engaged Cedric Dicksee to design and develop an oil engine. Dicksee remained at AEC until the 1950s, attaining a position of great eminence. Whether or not it was his decision to use the Acro air-cell combustion system (the licensor of which was also Bosch) he undertook the basic design of the A155 engine, the first AEC diesel engine offered to the market. With a bore and stroke of 100mm and 142mm respectively, giving a swept volume of 8.1 litres, the AEC-Acro engine hit the first target of giving the same power, 95bhp at 2,400rpm, as Rackham's 100mm bore 6.1-litre petrol engine. To cope with the increased loadings the cylinder centres were increased from 135mm to 145mm, the diameter of the main bearings from 70mm

to 85mm and of the big-ends from 63mm to 75mm, although the bearing material was still white metal as used in the petrol engine. It being anticipated — rightly — that with the much higher cylinder pressures there might be more trouble with cylinder head gaskets, the camshaft was located in the crankcase, so that two cylinder heads each covering three bores could be used. The effect of these changes compared with the petrol engine was to require a longer bonnet, the radiator being some 4½in further forward (and consequently about ¼in higher). An offside bonnet or make-up piece of this length was fitted between the radiator and the cab scuttle giving vehicles fitted with this engine and its later derivatives their characteristic 'snout'.

The camshaft was driven by a triple roller timing chain which also drove the fan and two auxiliary shafts on the side of the crankcase. The upper of these was the half speed drive for the brake exhauster and fuel injection pump. The lower shaft drove the water pump (located in front of the timing case), the governor and two 7in dynamos in tandem. It will be noticed that the governor was not at this stage part of the equipment obtained from Bosch. It was designed by AEC and worked the fuel pump rack by an external lever and link.

In the AEC-Acro engine this governor only controlled idling speed. The engine was ungoverned as regards maximum speed, unlike every other design of diesel engine before or since. This was a bit of bravado on

Right:
The AEC-Acro oil engine, type A155, showing the Bosch fuel pump and upward-pointing injectors. The engine seen here is in goods vehicle trim with single 5½in dia dynamo; LGOC engines had two 7in dia dynamos driven in tandem. *Author's Collection*

the part of Rackham who, overriding the more cautious Dicksee, wanted to be able to claim for the AEC oil engine a speed range of 300rpm to 3,000rpm. However, if the throttle pedal (as it was still called) stuck in the open position there was nothing to prevent the engine attaining a destructive speed.

Besides ST462, 464 and 466, AEC-Acro oil engines were fitted in three coaches, T216, 274 and 305, licensed in February 1931, and nine LT-type buses, LT191-199, licensed in April. In all cases the Public Carriage Office permitted the extra length without any dimensional alterations to the body, although the seating capacity of the three ST-type vehicles was reduced to 44. This was necessary for compliance with the laden weight restriction of 9½ tons then still applying to two-axle buses; naturally the oil engine itself was heavier and additional weight also resulted from the brake exhauster and the two dynamos and bigger batteries which went with the 24V system. This in turn was needed to start the engine with its 19:1 compression ratio, 8.1-litre capacity and heater plugs.

In all these installations the axle ratio used was the same as had been used for comparable vehicles fitted with 100mm bore petrol engines, viz 6.25:1 for the ST-type and T-type vehicles and 8.33:1 for the LT-type. When we come to the two latter series we shall see that the petrol-engined examples had 110mm bore engines with which a higher axle ratio was used; consequently the oil-engined vehicles appeared under-powered in comparison. The improvement in fuel consumption was also disappointing — about 7mpg for the LT-type buses, compared with an average of five for those with petrol engines. More important than either, however, was the propensity of the AEC-Acro oil engine to disastrous failures. The call for replacement engines under warranty shortly began to absorb the whole output. Something had to be done.

Faced with this situation, Rackham allowed Dicksee to invoke the help of Ricardo & Co of Shoreham. The result was a transformation of the engine in an astonishingly short space of time — just what was needed, in fact. Ricardo designed a new combustion system, known as the Comet (subsequently known as the Comet Mk 1; later derivatives are still used today). This meant a new cylinder block as well as new heads and the opportunity was taken to increase the bore from 110mm to 115mm, making the swept volume 8.85 litres. The compression ratio was reduced to 16:1; the original crankshaft and crankcase were retained but the bearing material was changed from white metal to lead bronze. Most important of all, the governor was redesigned to control not only idling but maximum speed. This was initially set at 2,400rpm, at which the engine was now rated at 130bhp — an increase of 37% on

the AEC-Acro engine. Such was the improvement in air utilisation obtainable with the new combustion system, it was shortly found that the fuelling could be increased to give this power at only 2,000rpm.

This was a period when the oil engine was attracting great interest in the bus industry, and it was the subject of a special meeting arranged by the Municipal Transport & Tramways Association at Manchester in September 1931. The first AEC-Ricardo engine was hurriedly built into LT643, one of a further batch of LT-type double-deckers then being built, and driven off to Manchester for demonstration at this meeting. Also making their first appearance at the same meeting were the first Leyland oil engines, some examples of which were to be fitted in Leyland buses belonging to independents later taken over by London Transport, and the 6LW six-cylinder Gardner engine. Specially designed for transport applications by this Manchester firm which had previously aimed its products exclusively at the marine and industrial markets, the Gardner engine was of the direct-injection type (as was the Leyland although the combustion system was quite different). The specific fuel consumption claimed for the Gardner engine was some 11% less than that of the AEC-Ricardo engine and this attracted the interest of the LGOC.

Thus it was that the Gardner engine which was fitted in LT1051 came to be ordered. The Gardner engines were bulky, in particular being long and having a large diameter flywheel, so they were not easy to accommodate. The length was due to the incorporation of bearings of generous size (these were lined with white metal) and a mechanical crankshaft damper housed within the crankcase. They were of a modular design, with the option of four, five or six cylinders and a common rating of 17bhp per cylinder at a governed speed of only 1,700rpm. To get barely more than 100hp one had to have the six-cylinder engine, but it needed a bonnet practically 5ft long. The LGOC had two buses with bonnets of this length, LT1000 and 1051; undoubtedly that is why one of these was chosen as the test vehicle and as we have seen, it was a bad mistake when it was decided that the alterations to the chassis needed to accommodate a six-cylinder engine were too great and a five-cylinder engine was ordered instead.

The engine supplied, in November 1931, was actually the first 5LW engine built. After the experience in LT1051 (related in the previous chapter) a deal was struck in May 1932 whereby the five-cylinder engine went back to Gardner and the LGOC received a six-cylinder engine; this was fitted in an AEC Renown chassis, LT741, which as we shall see had previously carried a prototype body of new design. The installation of this engine, almost certainly undertaken at AEC, seems to have been governed more by considerations of convenience than of achieving a compact result; the bonnet length eventuating was 5ft 2¼in, which impelled the LGOC to build a new body for LT741, specially shortened at the rear, before offering it to the Public Carriage Office for recertification. Within a couple of years 5LW engines were being shoehorned into the existing (4ft 4⅞in long) bonnets of quite a large number of Regents belonging to companies in the Tilling group, but these conversions probably involved some redesign of the flywheel and clutch housing and also ran without fans — something made possible by the low heat rejection of the Gardner engine but which may not have been appreciated in 1932 when LT741 was converted. A similar installation of the six-cylinder engine would have fitted within a bonnet length of 4ft 11⅛in.

With its six-cylinder Gardner engine and new body, LT741 was ready for return to traffic in August and it was then sent to Hanwell to join the other oil-engined buses there. With an axle ratio of 5.75:1, it had a top speed of about 34mph.

Reverting to the AEC-Ricardo engine, the unit fitted to LT643 was the first of 20 oil engines of the new type which were specified in the sanction for 450 LT-type buses built between July 1931 and January 1932. The remaining 19 engines were fitted in LT750-768, placed in traffic between November 1931 and January 1932. All the former AEC-Acro (A155) engines were then reworked to the new specification, whose unit code was A161. As fitted in the LT-type buses, including three, LT948, 949 and 590, which received the engines formerly fitted in ST462, 464 and 466, the axle ratio used was now 6.75:1 — the same as that used in their sisters with 110mm bore petrol engines. In the three coaches T216, 274 and 305, however, the axle ratio was kept at 6.25:1, the ratio used with the 100mm bore engine, and it was, surprisingly, maintained at this value until T216 was converted to 11T11 and T274 and 305 were sold.

Happily, the AEC-Ricardo engine was now completely successful. The fuel consumption of the LT-type buses fitted with it averaged 8.4mpg. Although this was not as good as that of the buses fitted with Gardner engines, which eventually numbered 11 the LGOC were now very satisfied with the mix of reliability, economy and performance which the AEC-Ricardo engine offered. For subsequent production AEC redesigned the 8.8-litre engine fairly extensively. The most obvious changes were that the governor was now incorporated in the fuel pump, which in turn was made in Britain under licence by CAV Ltd, and the two 7in engine-mounted dynamos previously used were replaced on chassis for the LGOC by a single 8in machine mounted under the saloon floor and driven by a long universally jointed shaft from the timing case. However, there were also other changes, including repositioning some of the studs which secured the cylinder block to the crankcase, which had the effect that when a direct-injection conversion was later made for the A165 engine (as the 1932 design was known) it could not be applied to the A161 engine. The 32 LT-type buses fitted with the earlier type engines thus survived without further alteration, save for a reduction in the governed speed to 2,000rpm, until their withdrawal in 1949. Presumably the number of these engines left in service in 1938 was not considered to justify producing a special conversion. That produced for the A165 engine involved a new cylinder block as well as cylinder heads and alterations to the fuel pump and injectors. Most AEC oil engine designs of the 1930s were destined to appear in two or three versions.

Developments were, meanwhile, taking place in other fields besides engines. Another important area where progress was badly needed was the transmission. In practically all motor vehicles in the 1920s this consisted of a dry friction clutch and crash gearbox. There were two principal exceptions. One was the Model T Ford, famous in the realm of cars and light vans; this used a planetary transmission controlled by two pedals worked by the left foot, but it only gave two speeds and when the Model T went out of production in 1927, it was succeeded by a model with a crash gearbox and clutch. The other exception was found in the Tilling-Stevens buses used in London and elsewhere, which was an electric transmission consisting of a generator and motor. This gave a stepless drive but whilst it was completely foolproof, it was expensive and heavy. The lot of the vast majority of bus drivers was to change gear on a crash gearbox something like 2,000 times a day. The consequence for the LGOC was that in 1930, when Walter Gordon Wilson's preselective epicyclic gearbox made its appearance, neither the clutches nor gearboxes of buses could be relied upon to last in service for a year.

The gearset used by Wilson employed four simple epicyclic trains, each consisting of a sun wheel, planet carrier and annulus, interconnected in such a way that the indirect gears were each obtained by applying a band brake to one member of the appropriate train — the annulus in the case of reverse, first and second gears, the sun wheel in the case of third. Top gear was obtained by engaging a clutch between the input shaft and the third gear drum. All the gears were thus engaged frictionally and so the gearbox was crashproof. It had two controls; one, worked by the driver's foot, compressed the spring which applied the band or clutch selected; the driver's hand control determined which gear would be engaged next time the pedal was depressed and released. The gearbox was therefore preselective. An ingenious mechanism allowed the clamping load, which was different for each band, to be set to the

Left:
ST466 at Golders Green in 1931 after its transfer to Harrow Weald and now fitted with windscreen.
C. F. Klapper

Left:
The former T305 seen in 1947 after being sold by London Transport the previous year. For this purpose its body was exchanged with that from T120 which had been converted to a staff ambulance early in the war. This conversion involved making a new rear emergency door for bringing in stretchers, filling in the original rear passenger door and forming a new two-leaf folding door at the front of the saloon. When the bodies were exchanged the fuel tanks on both vehicles had also to be transferred to the opposite sides. As sold T305 still had its original-type A161 AEC-Ricardo 8.8-litre engine. *Author*

correct value and once set, maintained it at this value as the lining wore. Practically every detail of Wilson's design, much of which survives in gearboxes built today, showed similar ingenuity. A mechanical interlock made it impossible for two gears to be engaged at once.

It will be understood from the foregoing that the foot control resembled the clutch in an orthodox transmission; one could use it to slip the band for starting from rest, and the Wilson gearbox was thus a complete transmission. This was in fact how it was used in its first application when it appeared as an option in the 1930 Armstrong Siddeley car models. Armstrong Siddeley manufactured these gearboxes itself, becoming Wilson's first licensee.

Wilson's next licensee was Daimler. Here, however, Pomeroy, the Chief Engineer (whom we met in Chapter 1) saw the advantage of combining Wilson's Self-Changing Gearbox with the Fottinger fluid coupling, which was then being promoted in Britain by an engineer named Sinclair. Although both gearbox and fluid coupling were patented separately Daimler obtained a patent for using the two in combination as a vehicle transmission. As the casing of the fluid coupling formed the engine flywheel, Daimler coined the name fluid flywheel and the transmission became the Daimler fluid flywheel transmission or, more briefly, Daimler fluid transmission. The Daimler Co made not only cars but buses, and in the autumn of 1930 they offered the new transmission on both. The first bus model on which it was offered was a new model introduced in 1930 and known as the CG6 which became the CH6 with fluid transmission. In double-deck form the new chassis was shorter in the wheelbase than the previous CF6 model, the wheelbase (quoted at 15ft 6⅝in) being effectively the same as that of the AEC Regent, whose neat front end design it also copied. The new chassis was clearly designed with an eye to capturing some of the market being enjoyed by the AEC Regent, which had already become the market leader amongst double-deck bus chassis, and it succeeded in capturing the interest of the LGOC, which ordered three chassis soon after the new models were announced. The chassis in question were numbered 9023-5, the CG6/CH6 series having begun at 9001. The LGOC gave them the numbers DST 1-3.

Undoubtedly the feature of the CH6 chassis which must have appealed least to the LGOC was the 97mm by 130mm sleeve-valve engine. Barely a year had elapsed since engines of this type which had been fitted in nine of the 12 LS-type buses as first built in 1927-28 had been replaced with AEC overhead camshaft engines at their first overhaul. When in 1931 Daimler began offering a poppet-valve engine, 103mm by 130mm, based on the same crankshaft, the LGOC bought one of these engines which they fitted in DST3 in March 1932, but evidently did not think well enough of it to convert DST1 and 2 similarly, nor of the rest of the chassis design to fit AEC engines to all three.

Turning to the transmission, which was really the feature for which the LGOC had bought the CH6 chassis, the gearbox was mounted separately amidships. At the time the chassis for the LGOC were built, Daimler was still feeling its way with the new transmission; the fluid flywheels fitted to the LGOC examples were of two different sizes and the gearboxes, according to a note on the rolling stock cards for these vehicles, were built by Armstrong Siddeley. Wilson had designed the gearbox with alternative gearsets giving wider or closer gear ratios, the difference being obtained by using either a 20 or 26-tooth sunwheel for first and second gears and adjusting the planet trains accordingly. For the CH6 chassis with its rather weak sleeve valve engine of only 5.7 litres the wide ratio set was adopted; this gave forward ratios of 5.1, 2.82, 1.66 and 1.0:1, top gear being direct via a cone clutch. The alternative close ratio gearset was adopted the following year for the CP6 chassis with its 6.5-litre poppet valve engine; this gave ratios of 4.15, 2.36, 1.48 and 1.0:1. These ratios were also used for the gearboxes which Daimler were to supply to AEC between 1931 and 1934. In the Daimler chassis the selector control took the form of a right hand quadrant mounted on the steering column, the same arrangement as Daimler used in most of their cars although in Armstrong Siddeleys and some Daimler cars it was on the left.

The chassis of DST1-3 were delivered to Chiswick in December 1930, just about the

time that the first three oil-engined buses were being got ready for service. They were bodied during January 1931 using three of the ST2-type bodies, suitably modified, then being built for ST518-817. At the beginning of February the three completed buses entered service at Harrow Weald. They were used on Route 18 which worked between there and London Bridge. At this stage they did not have windscreens, which were not approved by the Public Carriage Office for universal fitting until March. Thus whereas the oil-engined LT191-9 which entered service at Harrow Weald in April had windscreens from new, DST1-3 did not receive windscreens until September.

With the exception of the transmission the LGOC did not take to the Daimler chassis which were destined to have a very short life in London service. The three LGOC CH6 chassis, which had nearside fuel tanks, together with a fourth taken over from an independent, DST5, which had an offside fuel tank, were all sold in 1935 although (as related in a later chapter) the bodies of all four were retained for reuse on new short-wheelbase chassis specially ordered from AEC. However, the transmission did all that was claimed for it. Undeniably it was an enormous advance on the friction clutch and crash gearbox then being fitted with no other option in AEC chassis. The fluid flywheel gave faultless take-off from stops. The crash-proof gearbox action made it possible to change up from first to second gear on steep uphill starts where with a crash gearbox it was impossible. The new transmission offered real hope of a substantial improvement in overhaul life compared with the AEC clutch and D119 gearbox. To the drivers the preselective control brought the ability to change gear when both hands were occupied, something which they quickly learnt to use to advantage.

When DST1-3 entered service so impressed was the LGOC by the transmission that it called for Daimler transmission to be fitted to three AEC chassis of the batches then being delivered, one Regent (ST746) and two Renowns (LT439 and 448). For the AEC installation Wilson designed a gate-type selector which was mounted on a pedestal attached to the engine in place of the ordinary change-speed control used with the crash gearbox. This gate took the form of a staggered H, in which there were long movements for first and top gears and short ones for second and third gears. This meant a different selector camshaft in the gearbox as neutral and the intermediate gear positions came in a different sequence, but otherwise the gearbox was the same as that described for the Daimler CP6 chassis. It is likely that these first three installations were undertaken in the Experimental Department at AEC under Wilson's supervision. On delivery to Chiswick ST746 was given a body of the ST2-type and LT439 and 448

Chiswick-built bodies of the LT3-type then being built. All three bodies were modified in respect of having a large floor trap over the gearbox which was mounted amidships where, as in the Daimler chassis, it replaced the intermediate propshaft bearing. ST746 was allocated to Harrow Weald where it could run in comparison with DST1-3 but LT439 and 448 were sent to Plumstead, a garage serving a hilly part of southeast London. All three buses entered service at the beginning of June.

Unfortunately ST746 with its preselective gearbox is lost to sight after this. However, only two months later a further 20 LT-type buses (LT549-552, 566-571 and 583-592) with fluid transmission were sent to Plumstead. This equipment was specified in the sanction for LT501-950; it was fitted on the track in the factory at Southall and the Daimler gearbox now received an AEC production unit number, D128.

On 26 February 1932 LT590 was recalled to Chiswick, where the body was removed, and sent as a chassis to AEC. Here it was fitted with the last of the oil engines removed from ST462, 464 and 466 and now reworked from the A155 AEC-Acro to the A161 AEC-Ricardo specification. While the chassis was at AEC the body was modified to suit the diesel-engined chassis with its 24V electrical system and larger batteries. When they were reunited in March, LT590 made history by becoming the first bus in London to have fluid transmission and a diesel engine in combination. It was also destined to be the only oil-engined bus in London ever to run with a pedestal type selector, as this was superseded by an AEC-designed ball type selector beginning with 20 oil-engined buses built with fluid transmission in the summer of 1932. LT590 was not sent back to Plumstead but joined the other oil-engined buses then in service at Harrow Weald and with them was transferred to Hanwell the following month. The transmission equipment was later transferred into a petrol-engined chassis in which with a suitably adapted body it was sent back to Plumstead. LT590 continued to carry an oil engine after receiving a crash gearbox and like its 31 sisters was later grouped in LPTB chassis code 4LT. Its original body (12529) remained as one of those kept for this group of chassis although as there were enough of these to justify a dedicated spare, it did not always remain on LT590.

Hydraulic brakes came into widespread use on American cars in about 1930. The system used was developed by an emigrant Scottish engineer named Lochhead who adopted the trade name Lockheed to make it more easily pronounceable to Americans. In Britain the Lockheed system was promoted by its licensees, the Automotive Products Co of Leamington Spa. The advantage of hydraulic operation was the ease with which correctly balanced and proportioned braking could be obtained. As applied to

AEC bus chassis, the master cylinder was originally fitted behind the servo; it was later made integral with it. The slave cylinders for the rear brakes were frame-mounted, but those for the front were machined in the hollow kingpins of the front axle.

The first LGOC vehicle to have been so equipped seems to have been a Regal chassis, 662803, one of three originally intended for the East Surrey Traction Co in 1931 for use as buses which later became T380-382 in the London Transport Country Area fleet. This chassis was exchanged with one of a batch of 100 coach chassis being built for the Green Line at the beginning of 1931 and became T220. The card raised for the latter in 1931 referred to it as having Lockheed brakes but the later card raised by London Transport in 1935 did not. Presumably T220 had been converted to the standard triple servo-mechanical system meanwhile.

The next LGOC application of hydraulic brakes was a conversion applied to 10 T-type buses in May and June 1931. Apparently the equipment was stripped out of the chassis when they next came through Chiswick for overhaul with the result that between the following October and December five of the chassis originally converted ceased to be so equipped and five other chassis were equipped instead so that there were still 10. These vehicles retained this equipment for the rest of their lives.

In January 1932, LT673 was placed in traffic at Plumstead with Lockheed brakes. This was obviously a prototype of the system it was intended to apply to 50 buses of the Bluebird series in which it was paired with fluid transmission. These included 30 with petrol engines, LT1325-1354, which were sent to Plumstead in June and July. Here again, the hydraulic brakes and transmission equipment were removed from the first five of these buses and transferred into LT964 and 1235-1238 at dates between July 1933 and August 1934. The hydraulic brake equipment was removed, permanently, from LT673 at its first overhaul.

LT1355-1374, built in the summer of 1932, introduced the combination of oil engine, fluid transmission and Lockheed brakes which was to become standard in London Transport buses built between 1934 and 1939. The AEC-designed ball type selector which made its first appearance in these buses superseded the Wilson-designed pedestal type in chassis with fluid transmission supplied by AEC from then on. In appearance this resembled a slightly miniaturised normal gear-stick, with a flattened knob. The gate was still of the staggered H-type and the movements transmitted to the gearbox were unchanged. The gearbox itself was still the Daimler-built D128 unit. Practically another two years were to elapse before buses with AEC-built Wilson gearboxes began to appear in service.

6: The LGOC ST, T and LT Types, 1931-32

In the autumn of 1930 when the AEC Regent, Regal and Renown chassis had been in production for about a year various specification changes were introduced. Worm and nut steering replaced the Marles unit; triple servo brakes became standard on the four-wheeled chassis as well as the Renown; the D119 gearbox was replaced by the D124, with constant-mesh third gear. A 110mm bore version of the petrol engine, unit No A145, rated at 110hp, became available; although this was primarily aimed at the Renown, an axle ratio of 5.2:1 was introduced for use with it in the Regal. The most noticeable change was to the Regal which now had 20in wheels with low pressure tyres of a size later known as 9.00-20 (but then called 38×9) as standard.

Before we come to new orders placed for what may be termed 1931 specification chassis we have still to mention the 50 single-deckers on long-wheelbase Renown chassis, LT1001-50, outstanding from the original notice of intent given to AEC. These had been ordered against sanction 24/978 and the body Nos 10327-10376 had been allocated. However only LT1001 was completed in 1930, in December, following the conversion of T27 to front entrance and rear emergency door. In its general appearance the body was a longer version of T27 as reconstructed but the pillar spacing was increased to give a wider entrance, with the result that there was a short bay over the rear overhang. The pillars were also noticeably thicker than those of the T type bodies. Thirty five seats were accommodated within an overall length of 29ft 5in. The odd number was due to the transverse seats in the forward part of the saloon being

Below:
Single-deck LT1089 at Borehamwood, August 1934.
LT 18584

staggered to allow for the wider entrance; in the resulting layout there was a longitudinal seat for six over the offside rear wheels but one for only five on the nearside. Although LT1001 was licensed in January 1931 the remaining 49 buses did not appear until April. Most of this first batch were allocated to Muswell Hill. They had round-fronted cabs with windscreens, a destination box at the front only and seats of the square-backed type which had been used throughout 1930. With a licensing weight of 6ton 11cwt 3qr these buses used the 100mm bore engine with an axle ratio of 6.75:1, a specification which they and their later sisters retained until about 1950 when the survivors were given 7.7-litre oil engines from scrapped STLs. Thus equipped they lasted until 1952. As described they received the LPTB code 1LTL1.

Two spare single-deck bodies, one T-type (11543) and one LT-type (11544) were authorised by sanction 24/1039. The latter was completed in May, but the former, which had not been built by January 1932, was then cancelled.

A further 149 LT-type single-deckers were built during 1931. Sanction 24/1064 covered LT1052-1101 and 52 bodies, Nos 12387-12438. These were an exact repeat of LT1001-1050 and appeared in May. They were quickly followed by the first 50 buses of the next sanction (24/1094, covering LT1102-1201 and 103 bodies, 12927-13029). LT1102-1151 were completed in June, when 51 single-deck bodies were built. Of these, 12927-12952 were identical with the preceding bodies. However, 12953-12977 incorporated the round-backed seats used in the ST2 type bodies and were fitted with rear destination boxes. These bodies, which received the LPTB code LTL1/1, also had a fillet at each side of the front destination box which is often distinguishable in photographs.

The chassis of LT1137 was appropriated for use as an experimental double-deck coach for the Green Line services. For this purpose it was given a 110mm bore engine. The design of the body, 13029, which was also completed in June 1931, obviously gave Chiswick a good deal of trouble. The same pillar spacing was used as in the single-deck bodies but both chassis and body were shortened at the rear where the short last bay of the single-deck design was

Below:
LT1137, working from St Albans in 1939, as reworked in 1935 with bus-type destination box, doorless entrance and front staircase. *D. W. K. Jones*

suppressed altogether. The entrance occupied the foremost bay, as in the single-deck design and was originally doorless as it was not at first considered possible to incorporate a sliding door such as was used in the latest single-deck coaches. However, an external sliding door was later added, the nearside fuel tank (or at least the filler neck) being moved to a position further aft to make room for it. The staircase was originally over the offside rear wheels, but in 1935 it was moved to a position opposite the entrance. This move may have been allowed for in the original design as the top deck was abbreviated at the front so that there were no seats forward of the staircase in its new position. At the same time the door was removed the nearside fuel tank was restored to its original position and a bus-type front destination box was fitted. With a length of about 27ft 6in LT1137 seated 54.

It was still classified as a coach when transferred to LGCS with the Green Line fleet on 29 July 1932. However, it had been demoted to a bus before it came to the LPTB by whom it was coded 1/1LTL2 in 1935. LT1137 worked from Hatfield and (from January 1939) St Albans until the end of the war, when it was reportedly used as a test vehicle for a GM two-stroke oil engine before being scrapped in September 1946. It would undoubtedly have been more useful if it had been built as or even converted to a single-decker. The body originally incorporated a sliding roof, but this was later replaced by fixed panelling without altering its distinctive humped shape.

The remaining 50 single-deck buses, LT1152-1201, were turned out in September, when a further 51 bodies of the LTL1/1 type, 12978-13028, were built.

Reverting to the autumn of 1930, some 300 further ST-type buses were needed in the first six months of 1931 to complete the replacement of the K-type. ST518-817 were accordingly ordered against sanction 24/1032 with bodies 12010-12309, to which 15 spares were later added (12340-12354) as none had been included in the sanction for ST302-501. In the event no body was built with the number 12309, no doubt because the Metro-Cammell body 11535 had been ordered without any corresponding chassis.

These bodies incorporated seats of a new design, rounded at the back. The seating layout in the lower saloon was also altered without changing the seating capacity which remained at 49. Twenty-five bodies were again contracted to Strachans and 17 to Short Bros. Delivery began at the turn of the year. Buses licensed from March onwards had windscreens from new. As described these bodies received the LPTB code ST2.

The chassis of ST518-817 incorporated the new steering, brakes and gearbox alterations but retained the 100mm bore engine, 6.25:1 axle ratio and nearside fuel tank. ST746, licensed in June, was chosen for an experimental installation of the Wilson gearbox and fluid flywheel. Another exception was the body 12037, in which the staircase was moved backwards to the side of the platform, resulting in a gain of two seats downstairs and the loss of one upstairs.

Construction of the buses on this sanction overlapped with 24/1046, covering the Daimlers DST1-3; 24/1047, covering 15 further ST-type buses, originally intended for Overground (now an LGOC subsidiary) which were numbered ST822-836, and 24/1051, covering four ST-type buses,

ST818-821, for the National services at Ware. For the first two of these sanctions, 18 bodies, 12310-12327, were authorised and for the third the four bodies authorised were numbered 12920-12923. These bodies were all needed to complete these vehicles and although this is probably the order in which they were built, it is not how they were used for the respective chassis. The Daimlers, for instance, received bodies Nos 12078-12080 and ST822-836 and ST818-821 were also given bodies from the main series 12010-12308. The last LGOC chassis to enter service received the bodies 12920-12923 — one of these going on ST746, with its Wilson gearbox, which required a special floor trap. In body 12327 the front destination box was incorporated in the cab canopy. This was a try-out of the arrangement to be adopted in the LT5-type bodies built in the second half of 1931. The 15 spare bodies were numbered 12340-12354; the first five of these were built in June but the final 10 which were not built until September, also had the front destination boxes incorporated in the cab canopy. The very last body, 12354, also had the revised staircase position as used in the earlier body 12037.

This was not the final word in the story of General ST-type. There were also 30 buses built by Short Bros for the ESTC in the spring of 1931, 28 of which were provided by the LGOC and hence appeared on an LGOC sanction, 24/1055, and had LGOC body numbers, 12359-12386. A further LGOC sanction, 24/1056, which covered the purchase for the ESTC for four of the Regents bought the previous year for Autocar, has already been mentioned (Chapter 3). With the exception of ST1051, which was destroyed in a fire in 1933 without ever carrying that number, these buses came to the LPTB, receiving the numbers ST1040-1069 and 1085-1088 respectively in the 1935 numbering.

Before Overground received all of ST822-836 there was a change of plan in which it was decided instead to buy for them 25 Dennis Lances with Metro-Cammell metal framed bodies; these were ordered on sanction 24/1084. Two of the ST-type buses, ST833 and 834, were transferred to the ESTC at the beginning of April. The timing of this occurrence coincided with the transfer to the ESTC of Crayford garage with five T-type buses and the Morden-Dorking route with five NS-type. Except when route transfer was involved buses provided for the ESTC were always bought new and ordered specially and the transfer of these two buses is thus something exceptional. The explanation appears to be that in the autumn of 1930 the LGOC had agreed to replace 32 LGOC-owned PS-type buses and considered that they had met this obligation by purchasing the four buses from Autocar and ordering 28 new ones. However, the ESTC had found work for the four ex-Autocar buses immediately and would not have been able to withdraw the 32 PS-type vehicles in the spring without 32 replacements. The situation appears to have been resolved by the ESTC and the General agreeing each to provide another two buses, a commitment which the ESTC met by adding two to the LGOC's order for 28 new buses and the LGOC by diverting ST833 and 834. An opportunity to transfer ST833 and 834 back to Central Area occurred in LPTB days when Q2 and 3 were transferred to Country Area in 1937, but ST819 and 820, two of the ex-National buses, were chosen instead. LGOC-pattern ST-type buses were still a common sight in both Central and Country Areas during most of 1949. The last were withdrawn from service early in 1950. ST821 survives as the preserved example of the ST-type in the London Transport Museum.

Another order placed in the autumn of 1930 was for a further 100 coaches for the Green Line services, T207-306. The sanction against which these coaches were ordered, 24/1034, included 100 bodies, 11795-11894, all of which were contracted to outside suppliers, 25 to Weymann, 25 to Ransomes and 50 to Duple. This arrangement reflected a need for considerable haste as it was desired to get further services established before the licensing procedures of the Road Traffic Act came into force at the beginning of March 1931. All 100 coaches were licensed between the beginning of January and the end of February. The bodies differed from the previous Green Line Regals in having seven bays of equal pitch, a sliding door at the front, a central emergency door in the rear and a seating capacity of 30. The overall length was still 26ft although this was exceeded by three which were fitted with oil engines. With these exceptions, the chassis had the new 110mm bore petrol engine with which the new axle ratio of 5.2:1 was used together with 38×9 tyres. This combination made these vehicles capable of 60mph and speeds approaching this figure were alleged in one or two prosecutions soon after they entered service. With such speed capability the provision of triple servo brakes, although now standard, was undoubtedly wise. To suit the front entrance body these chassis had offside fuel tanks. As described they were coded 1/7T7/1 by LPTB In 1935; by this time the standard specification for these vehicles had been changed to 100mm bore engine and 6.25:1 axle ratio. T232, which (reportedly following a fire) had been rebodied in April 1933 with a rather clumsy-looking Weymann metal-framed body, was coded 1/7T7/2.

The three exceptions, T216, 274 and 305 were fitted when new with AEC-Acro oil engines with which an axle ratio of 6.25:1 was used. They originally worked on the High Wycombe route from what later became the railcar shop in the AEC works at Southall. This allocation was still shown on the record cards when the Green Line coaches were transferred to the LGCS on

29 July 1932; however, when new cards were raised at Chiswick in 1935 these three coaches were allocated to Reigate. The engines, like the AEC-Acro engines fitted to LGOC double-deckers, were converted to the AEC-Ricardo A161 specification early in 1932. Unfortunately the information from the rolling stock cards is rather incomplete — totally so in the case of T216, whose original card did not even acknowledge that it had an oil engine. That for T274 contained an undated later entry altering the bore from 110mm to 115mm and the rated power from 95 to 130bhp, indicating rework of the engine to the AEC-Ricardo specification. T305, however, had entries recording that it was back at Chiswick on 16 December 1931; its body (11844) was removed two weeks later; as a chassis it was moved to Reigate on 24 February and subsequently Southall, meaning AEC; and finally on 15 March 1932 with a 115mm bore engine it was fitted with body 11808 removed from T268 and relicensed. The card for T268 only contained the bald statement that the body was removed on the same date and the chassis dismantled. It is possible to believe that in the circumstances prevailing at the time AEC may not have been able to supply reworked engines on an exchange basis and that fitted to T305 in March was probably one of the last of the LGOC's AEC-Acro

engines to be reworked. However, this does not explain why the body 11844 should have disappeared without trace or why T268, barely a year old, should not have been given a new body. I can recall when I was at AEC in the 1950s hearing a tale of one of these coaches suffering a disastrous engine failure in Uxbridge Road, Southall, involving a pool of oil and metallic fragments, but even if this was T305 it would not account for the body becoming a total loss. By inference the event which befell T305 in December was something like an overturning accident or a fire.

These three coaches were given the code 2/7T7/1 by the LPTB in 1935. The new cards showed them as retaining the 6.25:1 axle ratio, suggesting that the engines were considerably derated after conversion. In December 1938, T216 was converted to 11T11 (see Chapter 11) and T274 and 305 were reclassified as buses. These two vehicles were sold in January 1946.

The coaches of the T207-306 series were scheduled for replacement by new 10T10-type vehicles (actually the 34-seaters of code 10T10/1) in 1938, and towards the end of that year T208, 212-216, 223, 226, 232, 234, 236, 237, 250, 253, 255, 261, 266, 267, 271, 275. 276, 280, 283, 285, 296, and 298 were converted to 11T11 specification with 1935 Weymann bodies removed from

Below:
T220, one of the third order for Green Line coaches placed in service in January and February 1931. When new this particular vehicle had Lockheed brakes.
LT U13351

55

R-type Reliances and 7.7-litre oil engines. These vehicles survived until 1952-53. Some others were downgraded to country buses without conversion and these were fitted with standard single-deck front destination boxes. However, others were retained on Green Line duty until the arrival of the TF-type in 1939; 25 petrol-engined T-type coaches are shown in the London Transport official return at 30 June 1939 (Appendix 2). Most of these vehicles were still in stock at the outbreak of war in September and were then converted to ambulances. At the end of the war they were coverted to country buses; they were thereafter distinguishable from the vehicles downgraded in 1938 by a different and neater arrangement of the front destination box, which in the postwar conversions occupied the space of the former single-line blind and the illuminated sign below it. The majority of these vehicles survived without other alteration until 1949.

Another requirement scheduled for 1931 was the replacement of the S-type. This was the part for which the CC-type had originally been cast, but in the autumn of 1930, when only two buses had been completed, it was looking increasingly improbable that the CC-type would be available in time to meet this need. An order was therefore placed with AEC for 350 short-wheelbase Renowns, LT151-500, for completion in the first half of 1931. Although effectively forming a single order, there were two sanctions, 24/1033 covering 100 chassis and 110 bodies (11895-12004) to be built at Chiswick and 24/1038 250 chassis with bodies to be built by outside contractors, 90 (11545-11634) by Park Royal, 80 (11635-11714) by Strachans and 80 (11715-11794) by Short Bros.*

The first buses were completed for licensing at the beginning of January 1931. With the exception of LT191-199 they had A145 110mm bore petrol engines with which the axle ratio used was 6.75:1. The bodies were of a straightforward inside-stair design, very similar in layout to the General STs with a full-width loading platform but with six bays between lower saloon bulkheads. Happily the design awkwardnesses of the CC-type body were eliminated, the same pillar spacing being carried right through to the rear quarter panels. For some reason however this was reduced from the 36in of the outside-stair bodies to 35¾in, a trifling alteration which destroyed the commonality of such things as glass, window frames and panels with the earlier outside-stair bodies but which nevertheless became the standard for all further LT double-deck bodies. Another unexpected decision had the effect that the seats were of

the type used in 1930 and not of the new curved back type used in the ST2 bodies being turned out at the same time. Whilst the body factory at Chiswick were no doubt used to such contradictions, this one must have seemed perplexing to Strachans and Short Bros who were building some of both types. Compared with the ST1/1-type body with the same type of seats the extra downstairs seats in the LT3 body (to give its later LPTB code) were all longitudinal, of which there were five instead of four on the nearside and two (as against none) on the offside. Upstairs there was one more row of transverse seats. Relative to a weight of just on eight tons the capacity of 56 was not such good value as either the 49 of the ST design or the 60 of the outside staircase LT.

One of the Chiswick bodies, 11957, was built with a prominent tumblehome to the upper deck windows and domed rear quarter panels; both these features were incorporated in the LT5-type bodies of the following order. This body, however, had them in more pronounced degree and it had the old type destination box and seats. It received the LPTB code LT4.

* Sanctions 24/1034 and 24/1038 between them included 15 spare bodies to cover the 500 LT-type buses so far authorised. All of these were built at Chiswick, five of them (12005-12009) being of the outside-stair type. Although numbered last, these were in fact built first to be available for the overhaul of LT2-50 January/February 1931.

Chiswick-built bodies were also fitted to all the chassis of this batch which incorporated special features. These included LT191-199, which entered traffic in April at Harrow Weald with AEC-Acro oil engines. As mentioned in the previous chapter, the engines were converted to the A161 AEC-Ricardo specification in the early months of 1932 when the chassis became common with LT590, 643, 750-768, 948 and 949. Also in common with the latter, from April 1932 onwards they operated from Hanwell until transferred to Mortlake in 1935. The nine bodies originally fitted to LT191-199 became part of the group of 33 reserved for the chassis of code 4LT in London Transport days becoming spread around these 32 chassis as a result. The LPTB coding of these bodies is discussed in Chapter 2.

LT439 and 448 were two of the first three AEC chassis fitted with fluid flywheels and Daimler-built Wilson gearboxes. The bodies fitted to these two chassis, 12003 and 12004, were the last two of the 110 LT3-type bodies built at Chiswick. These two bodies (which later received the LPTB code 3LT3/2) continued to be used for petrol-engined chassis with fluid transmission — the Plumstead preselectors — after all the 1931 crash-box chassis had been converted to oil in 1940 even though, as explained below, these were in most cases not then the original chassis thus equipped. The code LT3/2 was actually originated in 1934 when the fluid transmission equipment originally fitted to T307 and 308 was transferred into two petrol-engined buses of this series and two further Chiswick-built bodies, 11930 and 11933, were adapted to suit. From 1940 onwards these two bodies were on LT470 and 909, which were fitted with ball-type selectors — a consequence of the later origin of these two sets of equipment.

A further 450 chassis, LT501-950, were ordered in the spring of 1931 for completion in the second half of the year. The sanction for these, 24/1069, called for 20 of the chassis to be fitted with oil engines and 20 with Daimler transmission, the first mention of either of these things in a vehicle sanction. The sanction authorised the construction of 463 bodies, 12439-12901, all of which were to be built at Chiswick. They were in fact all completed between 23 June 1931 and 26 January 1932 — a remarkable achievement, considering that 51 single-deck LT and 10 spare ST bodies were also built during the autumn. Within the space of 14 months more than 860 double-deck and 200 single-deck bodies were produced at Chiswick.

Although the 463 bodies built against sanction 24/1069 included the first two Bluebirds, discussed shortly, the bulk were of a modified version of the 56-seat type built for the previous sanction. The upper deck windows were inclined inwards and the rear quarter panels domed, in the manner tried out in body 11957 although not in the same degree. The front destination box was incorporated in the cab canopy and seats of the curved-back type introduced in the ST2 bodies were used. As described these bodies were coded LT5 in the 1934 LPTB code system. The last 103 bodies, built in December 1931 and January 1932, were given a three-indicator-box arrangement at the front and an additional one at the rear: as fitted on petrol-engined chassis these bodies were coded LT5/1. Bodies of both types were fitted to the oil-engined chassis (codes LT5/3 and 5/4) and LT5-type bodies built with floor traps for the Daimler gearbox were coded LT5/2. Two bodies, 12599 and 12600, were appropriated for the third and fourth CC chassis,

Scene at Richmond in May 1939, showing examples of both variants of the 56-seat bodies built for the LT501-950 order.
LT U29714

LT1202 and 1203. This appropriation had already been more than made good by the three bodies 10480-10482 which had not been used for CC chassis for which they were built.

The chassis originally fitted with Daimler gearboxes and fluid flywheels were LT549-552, 566-571 and 583-592. The bodies for these were fitted with large floor traps over the midships-mounted gearboxes; this specification received the LPTB code 3LT5/2. These vehicles entered service at Plumstead in August or in the case of LT592, September 1931. The procedure adopted at Chiswick for the subsequent overhaul of these vehicles is interesting: there was no dedicated spare body with the large floor trap. The practice followed was apparently to remove the whole of the special transmission equipment from the chassis, which would then be refitted with either crash or fluid transmission depending whether an overhauled set of fluid transmission and a body with a trap to suit were both available. The usual effect was that a body which had previously been on a preselective chassis would emerge later from Chiswick on another with a higher number which had not previously had preselective transmission. However, it was obviously not a matter of great difficulty to cut out a midships floor trap in a standard body if the need arose, as it did for instance when the set of fluid transmission equipment was removed from LT590 and needed to be mated with another petrol-engined chassis and body to be sent back to

Plumstead. Production of LT151-950 originally extended over the whole 12 months of 1931, so that there were always vehicles of this type passing through Chiswick, with the result that bodies of the LT3, 5, and 5/1-types became spread haphazardly over these 800 chassis.

The migrations of fluid transmission equipment came to an end in 1940, when the last petrol-engined chassis with crash gearboxes were converted to oil. From then on the 24 petrol-engined preselectors were LT271, 401, 451, 469, 470, 571, 573, 580, 582, 588, 591-593, 649, 651, 652, 658, 659, 662, 786, 798, 827, 909 and 914. Of these, LT470, 592, 658 and 909 carried bodies of the LT3/2-type; the others were all of the LT5/2-type. LT571, 588, 591 and 592 probably carried preselective gearboxes throughout their lives. All the vehicles of this specification were always allocated to Plumstead for their whole lives which extended until 1949. Together with the 30 similarly equipped Bluebirds they formed a most distinctive group with the sound of the Daimler gearbox being prominently audible above the quiet engine. This was particularly the case when drivers idled in neutral, as they often did, and on restarting from rest, for which first gear was invariably used.

The 20 buses built with AEC-Ricardo oil engines as specified in the sanction were LT643 and 750-768. As mentioned in Chapter 5, LT643 was demonstrated at the Municipal Tramways & Transport Association conference in Manchester in Septem-

ber. The other buses were turned into traffic between November 1931 and January 1932 as engines and the related equipment became available. In consequence a relatively high proportion of the bodies fitted to these chassis were from the last 103 built with three separate destination indicators. When it was decided that the oil engines previously fitted to the three ST-type buses should after rework be transferred to buses of the LT-type, LT948, 949 and 950 were earmarked and held back at AEC. The last three 56-seat bodies of the batch built for the series, 12898-12900, were also held in readiness for these chassis and LT948 and 949 were duly turned into traffic in January and February 1932. When it was later decided to fit the last engine to LT590, as described in Chapter 5, the chassis of LT950 was released. It was fitted with one of the Bluebird bodies which were by this time in production and licensed in February. All the subsequent bodies fitted to LT950 were of the Bluebird type except one which it carried for a period between July 1937 and November 1938; it was converted to oil in February 1934. The body which had been prepared for LT950, 12899, was, after the necessary rework for use on a petrol-engined chassis, fitted to LT1232 on which it remained for a year.

A total of 169 chassis of the 1931 series (a convenient term for LT151-950) were converted to oil with AEC-Ricardo 8.8-litre engines of the later A165 type in 1933-34 in a programme which included all the petrol-engined Bluebirds except the 30 with fluid transmission. When petrol engines were required for the LTC-type coaches in 1937 a further 24 chassis were converted. These conversions were all coded 12LT. In 1939-40 the remaining 550 chassis which still had petrol engines and crash gearboxes were converted with a pot-type direct-injection version of the 8.8-litre engine; these conversions were coded 1/12LT. In both cases the axle ratio was changed to 5.75:1. Between 1940 and 1943 all the A165 type AEC-Ricardo engines fitted to the earlier conversions were converted to direct injection.

LT741 was completed in October 1931 with a special body, 12671, which turned out to be a landmark in London bus design. It exploited a new upholstery material, foam rubber, with a new design of seat framed in shaped plywood. At this date the standard upholstery material used in LGOC bodies was still curled hair (another instance, the reader may think, of reluctance by the LGOC to sever its last links with the horse) and as we have seen the weight of the seats used in the ST-type buses took them so close to the gross weight limit that some had to be removed in the three which were fitted with oil engines. The problem was not as severe in the case of the LT-type, which used seats of the same pattern, as the gross weight limit was more liberal and the standard 1931 design body only incorporated 56 seats. However, the LGOC had now apparently seen the point that if a two-axle bus weighing (laden) 9½ tons seated 49, a three-axle bus weighing 12 tons laden ought to seat at least 60.

To achieve a seating capacity of 60 the full-width loading platform and straight staircase were abandoned in favour of a corner staircase. This left room over the offside rear wheels for a seat for five, matching that over the nearside wheels and increasing the lower deck seating from 23 to 26. Upstairs, the adoption of a corner staircase meant a more extensive rearrangement and in the body built for LT741 the upper saloon was for the first time extended forwards for the full length of the cab. This eliminated the canopy used in all previous ST and LT-type bodies but the roof still overhung the upper deck front windows and central pillar. The staircase design adopted had no square landing and the last step at the top protruded through the bulkhead — an arrangement which was entirely unobjectionable in terms of bumped heads, achieved minimum intrusion into the platform and allowed a double seat upstairs to be placed right against the rear emergency window. Forward of this were two single seats, the inner of which fitted into the return of the staircase well. In front of this was another double seat on the nearside only and forward of this seven rows of double seats, giving a total upper deck seating capacity of 34.

This arrangement of staircase and seats was used in all Chiswick-designed rear entrance double-deck bodies until the RT-type. It gave a much better platform, staircase and passenger space at the head of the stairs than were found in the great majority of provincial double-deckers built during the next 20 years.

It would perhaps have been possible — just — to have built a bus with 60 seats of the earlier type which would have scraped within the 12-ton gross weight limit, but this would inevitably have weighed 8¼ tons unladen and would thus have left little or no scope for fitting oil engines. With the new seats, however, LT741 only weighed 7½ tons — a very worthwhile gain.

As first built, LT741 had single front and rear destination boxes of the type which had been current since LT1. Within a month of its completion, however, the LGOC at last woke up to the fact that all the double-deck buses it had built in the previous two years were seriously deficient in the amount of route information they conveyed to intending passengers compared with the board displays used on the NS-type. Accordingly

the new body on LT741 was provided with a much more comprehensive display. At both front and rear the original box was enlarged and devoted to a blind for intermediate points. Below this a single-line blind was added, that at the front for the ultimate destination only, that at the rear for this and the route number; and at the front only, a box for the route number was added to the front dome of the roof, hanging down slightly below it. The total effect was, for its day, a styling masterpiece such as few bus designs have achieved since. The Bluebirds made an impact hardly surpassed by the Feltham-type trams on people to whom a bus was just a piece of street furniture.

At this stage LT741 was upholstered in the ordinary lozenge design moquette used in the standard bodies then being built. The last body of the order for LT501-950, 12901, was built as a second prototype of the new design, presumably as a build prototype for the factory before they came to the bodies of the next sanction, 24/1115, covering LT951-999 and 1204-1404, in January 1932. This body was probably upholstered in the attractive blue moquette, like the production bodies which followed, which gave rise to the nickname Bluebirds by which these buses were always known.

The 250 chassis ordered against sanction 25/1115 were specified as 170 with petrol engines, crash gearboxes and triple servo brakes (originally LT951-999 and 1204-1324); 30 with petrol engines, fluid fly-wheels, Daimler gearboxes and Lockheed brakes (originally LT1325-1354); 30 with oil engines, crash gearboxes and triple servo brakes (LT1375-1404) and 20 with oil engines, fluid flywheels, Daimler gearboxes and Lockheed brakes (LT1355-1374). The LPTB codes allocated to these specifications in 1934 were respectively 5LT6, 6LT6/1, 7LT6/2 and 8LT6/3. The petrol engines were again of the A145 type 110mm bore with which an axle ratio of 6.75:1 was used. The oil engine were the new A165 version of the 8.8-litre AEC-Ricardo unit with which an axle ratio of 5.75:1 was used. The Daimler gearboxes were of the D128-type as fitted to the 23 earlier buses. The 30 petrol-engined buses with fluid transmission, which had pedestal-type selectors, joined the earlier buses with this transmission at Plumstead. The sanction included 258 bodies, 13087-13344.

LT1355-1374 were allocated to Hanwell, as also were LT1375-1404. The Plumstead buses entered service in June and July and the Hanwell buses between July and September. All the bodies, however, were completed before the works holiday at the end of July, including the spares, one of which (13341) was modified for use with the Gardner engine then fitted in LT741.

Despite the inclusion of Lockheed brakes in the specification of the petrol-engined buses with fluid transmission, some migration of equipment took place between these and the petrol-engined buses with crash gearboxes. The equipment was removed from LT1326, 1327 and 1329 on overhaul in May 1933, and from LT1325 and 1328 in November. LT964 was equipped with fluid transmission and Lockheed brakes in July 1933, LT1236 and 1238 in December, LT1235 and 1237 in July and August 1934. Presumably two other Bluebirds were also fitted with this equipment between July 1933 and July 1934. Fortunately for the historian these migrations came to an end after this as all the Bluebirds with crash gearboxes were converted to oil by mid-October, leaving LT964, 1235-1238 and 1330-1354 as the 30 petrol-engined preselective buses at Plumstead from then on.

The conversion of LT741 has been described in Chapter 5, but it is perhaps appropriate to repeat here that it resulted in the radiator being moved forward by no less than 9⅜in from its original position. Whether or not at the behest of the Public Carriage Office, it was considered necessary to fit a new body shortened at the rear by 3½in to keep the overall length down to 27ft 5in. In the standard Bluebird bodies, including the two prototypes, the rearmost bay had been extended to give more room to the platform and staircase. This resulted in the rearmost upper deck window on either side being noticeably wider than those between the lower saloon bulkheads which were at the 35¾in pillar spacing used in the 1931 bodies. To my eye this was one of the few visually unsatisfactory features of the Bluebird body design and in this respect the bodies produced to go with the Gardner engine were an improvement. The abbreviation of the rear end was accomplished without any sacrifice of seating capacity, although the uppermost tread of the staircase now protruded wholly forward of the lower saloon bulkhead.

Throughout their lives the Bluebird chassis were treated as a separate group from the LT-type chassis of the 1931 series. However, although in London Transport days they were distinguished by code from the earlier series, when I was at Chiswick in 1946 and able to examine them in their undressed state I was unable to discover any differences between chassis of codes 7LT (Bluebirds built with oil engines), 11LT (Bluebirds converted to oil in 1933-34), 12LT (1931 series converted to oil in 1934-37) and 1/12LT (1931 series converted to oil in 1939-40). By this time all the earlier engines in these chassis had been converted to direct injection.

This apparent sameness between the Bluebirds and 1931 chassis did not extend to the chassis of the outside-staircase buses dating from 1930 whose frames were

Below:
ST1070 (as it later became), one of the 23 Bluebird type buses built at Chiswick for LGCS in August 1932, at Watford in 1934.
J. F. Higham

62

Above:
LT1427 and 1428, the two Country Area single-deckers which made up the balance of the dowry for LGCS, at home in Dorking garage in July 1936.
LT U20848

noticeably longer at the rear (that on the offside being chamfered on the end). In this connection the code 1/2LT attached to the 1930 chassis, suggesting that the differences between these and the 1931 chassis only rated a sub-code when those between the 1931 chassis and the Bluebirds rated a whole code, may well have been a mistake, the intended code for these chassis really being 1/1LT. My belief that there was no difference of any significance between the 1931 and 1932 chassis is supported by the history of LT950 and 1232. Nothing seems to have hindered the fitting of a Bluebird body to the former chassis in February 1932 or a 1931-series body to LT1232 the following month, or of the opposite type of body to both chassis at a later stage. Between 1934 and 1937 LT910 also carried a Bluebird-type body, becoming the only petrol-engined bus with a crash gearbox to do so. During the war this body (13100) became one of those used for the petrol-engined Bluebirds with fluid transmission which had been left without a spare after the conversion programme on the crash gearbox examples ended in 1934. LT725 and 810 were fitted with Bluebird bodies in 1946.

On return from holiday in August 1932 the works set about building the bodies, numbered 13441-13465, for the 25 buses which LGCS received as a kind of launching present from the LGOC. Two of these were single-deck LTs on long-wheelbase Renown chassis for which the LTL1/1-type body design was used unaltered except for having the new type seats. These buses were later numbered LT1427 and 1428 and codes 2LTL3 by the LPTB. The other 23 buses were ST-type (ie 15ft 6½in wheelbase) Regents, the chassis of which were to the usual LGOC specification with nearside fuel tanks. An interesting detail which can be seen in early photographs of these buses is that they carried the AEC model name on the radiator, something which the LGOC would not have tolerated on chassis intended for their own use.

For these chassis a 25ft-long version of the Bluebird type body was produced, with the same arrangement of destination boxes and the same type of seats as the LT-type Bluebird bodies. However, the pillar spacing used in the earlier ST-type bodies was adopted and this was carried through to the bay over the platform, avoiding the visual awkwardness of the LT Bluebird body which I have mentioned. The last 25ft-long bodies to be built at Chiswick, they had a satisfying chunky appearance which I always liked better than that of the first STLs. Rather strangely, however, they were only provided with 48 seats. Of these, 22 were downstairs, as one would expect with removal of the staircase from the saloon to the platform. Upstairs there were only 26

63

seats, representing a removal of two rows compared with the Bluebird LT design. As the body was only 2ft shorter, this produced rather a sparse effect. The unladen weight of these buses was a bare 6 tons.

At this time a tidy-minded influence was at work at Chiswick and a batch of 25 registration numbers (GX5314-5338) was reserved for these 25 country buses. In the event, however, LGCS ran into difficulties after only 10 of the double deckers had been licensed* and the numbers GX5324-5336 were later used for STLs and two Dennis Darts. The same tidy-minded influence managed to get the registration numbers of LT1355-1374 and 1405-1426 in sequence with the bonnet and chassis numbers before the usual haphazard arrangement of allocating registration numbers as chassis were received was reverted to.

In September the remaining oil-engined buses of the main LT Bluebird order were

bodied, licensed and sent to Hanwell. Only one sanction, 24/1141, for 22 buses, LT1405-1426 with body Nos 13419-13440, remained to be completed before the LGOC abandoned three-axle buses for ever.

The first 12 of these buses, LT1405-1416, which were licensed and sent to Hanwell in October, had AEC-Ricardo A165 engines, crash gearboxes and triple servo brakes like LT1375-1404. However, instead of two 25gal fuel tanks they had a single 35gal fuel tank mounted on the offside and the batteries were moved to a position between the frame members. These changes were sufficient to ensure that the bodies for these 12 buses were wholly special and not interchangeable with the bodies of the oil-engined crash-gearbox examples of the main LT Bluebird order. When one of them was damaged by enemy action during the war one of the spares had to be extensively reworked to replace it and in due course the damaged body had to be reworked to serve as a spare for the standard chassis.

Why, one wonders, were these buses built with these modifications? They cannot have been of much benefit to the LGOC whose 1,200 other LT-type buses all had two fuel tanks — even LT741 and its Gardner-engined sisters which, experience was to prove, would have had the same range as the petrol-engined examples if one of the tanks had simply been removed. It was a

Below:
LT1423, one of 10 buses placed in traffic in November 1932 with Gardner 6LW oil engines, code 9LT7, on the model of the conversion applied to LT741 the previous July. It is seen at Grays in 1947 after these buses were removed from Hanwell. *Author*

* Of the remaining 13 buses, eight were later licensed by LGCS at Reigate and five at Ware in Hertfordshire. The effect was to split these buses into three groups when they came to be numbered by the LPTB in 1935 as all the previously unnumbered buses of the ST-type were numbered in order of their registration numbers. These 23 buses became respectively ST1070-1079, 1032-1039 and 1080-1084. All received the LPTB code 3ST4.

strange alteration to introduce in a small batch of buses which were to be the last of their type.

A conjectural answer to this question is that these chassis were a cancelled order for another operator which the LGOC took over. Is it possible that they were originally intended for LGCS, and that the Godstone Regents ordered the following year were a later substitution? The number of chassis was the same, the engine and transmission specification was the same and the modifications are consistent with front entrance bodywork. It is, of course, also possible that the LGOC may have contemplated building a small batch of double-deckers with front entrances for trial on its own services but abandoned this idea before the bodies for these chassis were built. LT1405-1416 received the LPTB code 10LT8.

LT1417-1426, which were licensed and sent to Hanwell in November, were the last LT-type buses to be built. They were an exact repeat of LT741 as converted in July, with Gardner 6LW engines, crash gearboxes, triple servo brakes and shortened bodies — further evidence to suggest that there was no real difference between the 1931 and 1932 chassis specifications. Coded 9LT7 by the LPTB, they remained at Hanwell until after the war except for LT1417 which was converted to an AEC 8.8-litre direct injection engine in 1945 and moved else-where. When at the end of 1946 the drivers at Hanwell decided that they had had enough of these buses with their low governed speed, low geared steering and strange throttle characteristic and refused to drive them any more, AEC 8.8-litre engines were found for four of them, which were moved to other Central Area garages, and the remaining six found a new home at Grays, in the Country Area, where the drivers were more compliant. The obvious possibility of appropriating the AEC 8.8-litre engines from STL1044-1055 and fitting the latter with new 7.7-litre engines, which were readily available and would have been common to the wartime 17STLs, seems not to have been considered. AEC 8.8-litre engines were eventually fitted to all but LT1420 and 1424 which alone carried their original Gardner engines until they were scrapped.

All the inside-stair variants of the double-deck LT-type were regarded as being interchangeable for operational purposes in LPTB days, and as such they were withdrawn in 1948-49. Almost the last to survive were some of the petrol-engined buses with preselective gearboxes at Plumstead, which also received six of the similarly-equipped oil-engined buses when these were displaced from Hanwell in May 1949. The last survivors, at Upton Park, were withdrawn in January 1950.

Below:
LT1413, one of the 12 buses of code 10LT8 placed in service in October 1932, at Marble Arch in May 1935. Note the absence of a nearside fuel tank. *LT 18111*

7: Other Vehicles of the ST, T and LT Types

The largest group of buses on AEC chassis of the new range introduced in 1929 which came to London Transport from sources other than the LGOC were the 191 Regents owned by Thomas Tilling Ltd which were operated from its garages at Bromley, Croydon and Catford. Built on standard 15ft 6½in wheelbase chassis with offside fuel tanks, these were of 1930 and 1931 vintages. The more recent ones had triple servo brakes and worm and nut steering from new and this specification received the LPTB code 2ST7. The chassis code 1/2ST was raised for any earlier chassis which had not been converted before coding.

The bodies of these vehicles were of Tilling design. As mentioned in an earlier chapter this clearly owed a certain amount to the Rackham-Short Bros demonstrator which Tilling received in July 1929, having an outside staircase and six bays between lower saloon bulkheads. It also had half-drop windows and a deep balloon roof. Most of these bodies were built by Tilling

itself in its works at Lewisham but some were built by Christopher Dodson at Willesden. The Dodson bodies of ST1029 and 1030 were similar in layout and used the same six-bay construction, and there were also noticeable similarities in the cab canopy. The Tilling buses were numbered ST837-1027 when the Tilling business was taken over by London Transport on 1 October 1933, whereupon the 195 bodies were numbered 13847-14041. By September 1939 Catford, their former principal stronghold, already had an allocation of standard STLs. With the outbreak of war services were immediately reduced throughout London Transport to save fuel, and particular attention was naturally given to the mileage worked by petrol-engined vehicles. Enough standard STLs were then moved into Catford to enable the Tilling STs at all three former Tilling garages to be taken out of scheduled service. Some became casualties during the war, a few were disposed of and others were lent to

Below:
Tilling ST-type bus at Victoria in April 1931, working from Bromley on Route 36. Note that Tilling used LGOC garage codes and running numbers. 191 buses of this type passed to the LPTB on 1 October 1933, becoming ST837-1027. *LT 17963*

undertakings such as Coventry which had suffered severely, but later in the war survivors began to reappear in service on short duties and rush-hour turns as well as driver training duties from garages which had never had them previously. Some could be found on Wimbledon specials as late as 1949.

Four buses, ST1028-1031 came to Central Area from independents. All had outside staircase bodies. ST1028 came from Chariot; it was a fairly early 1930 chassis, 661362, which was diverted from the first large General batch in which, had it not been diverted, it would have been ST154.

Consequently it had a nearside fuel tank. It had a 53-seat five-bay body by Birch Bros, with that builder's characteristic feature of the pillar spacing being different between the lower and upper saloons. ST1029 and 1030, which had consecutive chassis numbers, were both late 1930 or early 1931 chassis with offside fuel tanks and 54-seat six-bay bodies by Christopher Dodson; they came respectively from F. J. C. Kirk (Empire) and Pro Bono Publico. ST1031, which came from E. G. Hope (Pembroke), was a 1930 chassis with offside fuel tank, somewhat later than ST1028, like which it had a 53-seat five-bay Birch Bros body. All four vehicles,

Right:
ST1030, ex-Pro Bono Publico (PBP), with Dodson body, working from Camberwell at London Bridge after being taken over by the LPTB and still in PBP livery. *D. W. K. Jones*

Below:
ST1031, ex-E. G. Hope (Pembroke) with Birch Bros body at Caterham Valley in LPTB days. *D. W. K. Jones*

Left:
ST1089, ex-Amersham & District, with Short Bros two-gangway lowbridge body at Watford, 1947. *Author*

having bodies with a central opening front upstairs window, ran throughout their London Transport service with board displays and for most of this time were allocated to the former Tilling garage at Croydon. They were delicensed at the outbreak of war, being unusable in the blackout with externally illuminated displays. ST1028, 1030 and 1031 were in the air raid on Bull Yard in October 1940, in which ST1030 and 1031 were completely destroyed, but the chassis of ST1028 was salvaged and sold to the War Office for service as a Coastal Defence vehicle in December. ST1029 at that time was in store at Windsor, and as later in the war it was lent to and used by Rhondda Transport it was presumably converted to roller blinds. It was scrapped at Chiswick in June 1946.

ST1028-1031 were respectively coded 2/2ST8, 3/2ST8/1, 4/2ST8/2 and 5/2ST8/3 by the LPTB, as though the chassis all had more in common with the Tilling chassis, despite ST1028 having been built to an LGOC chassis specification; also the bodies of ST1029 and 1030, whilst distinguished by code, were effectively a pair.

The only Regents which came to London Transport's Country Area from a truly independent operator were six 15ft 6½in buses belonging to the Lewis Omnibus Co of Watford which became ST1133-1138. These buses originally had 48-seat six-bay inside-stair bodies by Short Bros. In common with all other highbridge 15ft 6½in Country Area Regents, except the 23 Bluebirds, they were coded 2/1ST9 by the LPTB In 1935. ST1133-1137 were quite early 1930 examples and their original Short Bros bodies, despite having inside staircases, bore some obvious resemblance to the 1929 Rackham-Short Bros demonstrators (of

which ST1139 was one). ST1138 was later, probably built about the end of 1930, and its body had some design differences, notably in the frontal treatment which was much less elegant but quite similar to the contemporary lowbridge body on ST1090. All six buses were rebodied by London Transport with spare ST-type bodies, ST1135/6/7 in 1939, ST1133/4/8 in 1942, some retaining their offside fuel tanks, some not, with no discernible pattern.

ST1089 and 1090 came from the Amersham & District Motor Bus & Haulage Co, in which the LGOC had a 50% stake. Of 1930 vintage, they both had 48-seat lowbridge inside-stair bodies of the same basic design as the six LGOC-owned National-operated buses mentioned earlier with which they shared the route between Chesham and Watford. Like the latter they received the LPTB code 3/1ST9/1, although these two buses had offside fuel tanks. The body on ST1089 was undoubtedly by Short Bros and survived to the end of its life with very little alteration, even retaining its cab door. The body on ST1090 is said by some authorities to have been built by Strachans, but it was of the same basic Short Bros design and by postwar years it had acquired a good deal of Chiswick top-dressing — waistrail mouldings and such like — as had all of the ex-National buses. Together with these, ST1089 and 1090 were fitted with 7.7-litre oil engines from scrapped STL-type buses in 1950 and survived until 1952, when they were replaced by new buses of the RLH-type.

The Regals inherited by London Transport which carried numbers between T307 and 402 formed a fascinating group and cannot be dealt with in a few lines. As we have seen above, the coaches built new to establish

Above:
ST1090, ex-Amersham & District, with two-gangway lowbridge body of Short Bros design, at Watford in 1936. *D. W. K. Jones*

Right:
ST1133, ex-Lewis Omnibus Co, with Short Bros highbridge body, West Croydon, 1936. *J. F. Higham*

the Green Line services received numbers up to T306 in the LGOC series which they carried throughout their lives. When the business of Buck's Expresses was taken over in February 1932 rolling stock cards were raised for the two Regal coaches acquired with that concern which were given body numbers (13366/7) although not, at this stage, bonnet (or type) numbers. On 11 May 1932, following the formation of London General Country Services in April, the 16 former East Surrey touring coaches were transferred to the Green Line fleet. This was while Green Line Coaches were administered directly by the LGOC and again, rolling stock cards were raised at Chiswick for these vehicles which were given LGOC body numbers (13403-13418) but not type numbers. When on 29 July the entire Green Line operation was transferred

Above:
ST1138, ex-Lewis Omnibus Co, with Short Bros highbridge body of later design, St Albans, 1935.
J. F. Higham

Below left:
T392 (T308 in the LGCS numbering), one of the two coaches inherited from Buck's Expresses with bodies clearly modelled on the Green Line front entrance design. (See also view on page 128.) *J. F. Higham*

to London General Country Services, the cards for T38, 51-155, 157-267, 269-306 and the 18 unnumbered Regals were marked 'sold to LGCS 29/7/32'.

When 12 Regal buses for the services operated by Thomas Tilling were ordered, they were allocated the numbers T307-318 which they were to carry throughout their lives. LGCS, however, knew nothing about these Tilling buses. However, it decided to continue to use the LGOC bonnet numbers for the Green Line coaches, and proceeded to give numbers to the T-type vehicles which did not yet have them, beginning with the unnumbered coaches transferred from the LGOC. These were numbered T307-324 (the two ex-Buck's Expresses being T307/8 and the 16 ex-East Surrey coaches T309-324). They then proceeded to number the 21 Autocar coaches T325-345. When the six Regals were taken over from Blue Belle with the London-East Grinstead route in August 1932 they were numbered T346-351. The six taken over from Queen Line with the London-Baldock route in April 1933 were numbered T352-357 and one from C. Aston of Watford in May became T358.

On the formation of London Transport on 1 July, T325-345, which were still the property of Autocar, passed to Maidstone & District. However, 10 other Regal coaches came to London Transport, four (T360/3/7/8) from the Lewis Omnibus Co of Watford (taken over on 1 October 1933) and six (T359/61/2/4/5/69 from Amersham & District (taken over on 24 November). Why the LPTB numbering of these vehicles was so haphazard is a mystery, when those numbered in LGCS days had been treated so methodically. It seems likely that T359-368 were given these numbers shortly after the

Above:
T346, one of the six coaches taken over from Blue Belle with the Marble Arch-East Grinstead route in August 1932. *J. F. Higham*

Far left:
T401 (T317 in the LGCS numbering), one of the ex-ESTC touring coaches of 1931, on Windsor Tour duty, Victoria Embankment, c1937. *D. W. K. Jones*

Left:
The former T338 in the LGCS numbering, one of the Autocar touring coaches of 1931 which passed to Maidstone & District on the formation of the LPTB, at Hanwell in 1947. Note that it has half-drop windows and also that it still has the original roof luggage rack, although reduced in height. *Author*

Amersham takeover and that in the process the numbers of T359 and 363 may have been transposed accidentally. However, the numbering of the buses which followed in 1935 was no better and not nearly so tidy as that of the Country Area Regent double-deckers. Two which came from the Watford Omnibus Co (taken over on 1 July 1933) were numbered T369 and 371; one which came from St Albans & District (in November 1933) became T370, and of the 19 former East Surrey buses which became T372-390, T372-379 were eight of the 16 1930 buses, T380-2 were the three Weymann-bodied front-entrance buses of 1931 and T383-390 the remaining eight 1930 buses.

When the Country Area engineering records (such as they were) were transferred to Chiswick on 25 February 1935 the duplication of the numbers T307-318 was discovered and the coaches carrying these numbers were then renumbered T391-402. The opposite choice, of renumbering the ex-Tilling buses, would actually have been a better one as that made had the effect of splitting the 1931 ex-East Surrey coaches into two groups. In the description which follows the LGCS numbering is used.

T307 and 308, first licensed in October 1931, were of interest in having 26ft long service coach bodies with front sliding door, rear emergency door and half-drop windows, the design of which clearly derived from that of T207-306. In the respects in which it differed from the latter, most notably a slightly higher build and front domes of the square shape used in Chiswick bus bodies (eg T369) it followed the three Battens' Reliances R35, 36 and 43 which were licensed at the beginning of March. It seems likely that these bodies were built by Weymann which had then just built 25 of the bodies for T207-306 and had no coach body design of its own. Weymann must have had access to Chiswick body drawings about this time to tender for the bodies for the three East Surrey Regal buses which became T380-382, even though when these came to be built in April and May the cab and front dome were an area where considerable liberties were taken.

T307 and 308 made ideal Green Line coaches. Upon the arrival of the 10T10-type in 1938, they were (by now as T391 and 392) downgraded to buses and fitted with standard bus type front destination boxes. By the end of the war T391 had had the passenger door removed and was operating in Central Area from Kingston, where it survived until 1950. T392, which still had its passenger door, was sold at the beginning of May 1945 to the Allied Control Commission in Germany.

T309-314, first licensed in March and April 1930, were ex-East Surrey touring coaches with 27ft long Hall Lewis folding-roof bodies seating 29. They had two passenger doors, both of the swing type, and full-drop windows, a combination which in 1930 evidently gained exemption from any need to have an offside or rear emergency door. With half-canopy cabs and a high waistline they were of very unattractive appearance. As T393-398 they were, with the exception of T396, sold in April/May 1938 following the arrival of the LTC-type coaches. T396 was fitted with an AEC 7.7-litre oil engine and ex-Reliance Weymann 1935 body in March 1938, becoming the first conversion to 11T11. Previously these six coaches had been coded 8T8/2 by the LPTB.

The Autocar coaches numbered T325-336 by LGCS were similar and clearly were ordered at the same time. The chassis numbers of the East Surrey and Autocar coaches were intermingled both with one another and with the contemporary buses

Above:
T363, one of two 1930 touring coaches with Harrington folding-roof bodies inherited from the Lewis Omnibus Co.
D. W. K. Jones

Above right:
T367, one of two 1932 coaches with Harrington bodies of later design with rear sliding door and rigid sliding roof, working as a country bus in early LPTB days.
J. F. Higham

Right:
T366, one of six coaches with Strachan bodies taken over from the Amersham & District Bus Co.
D. W. K. Jones

built for both companies, although the latter were only 26ft long.

T315-324, first licensed in March and April 1931, were ex-East Surrey touring coaches on 1931 specification chassis with triple servo brakes. They had 27ft long Park Royal folding-roof bodies of much improved design with a full-width canopy. Also seating 29, they had a front passenger door (still of the swing type) and an offside rear emergency door. With Green Line-style destination boxes and Chiswick-design round-fronted cabs, these were much better-looking bodies. However, the swing door was a liability for Green Line use and these vehicles were also sold or, in some cases, converted to service vehicles in April-May 1938. Despite being of 1931 chassis specification they were coded 8T8/1 by LPTB. The Autocar coaches numbered T337-345 were similar; view 64 shows one of them in service with a later owner with half-drop windows, but these may have been put in during their time with Maidstone & District. As far as is known all the East-Surrey coaches had full-drop windows. As in 1930, the East Surrey clearly ordered a batch of coaches for itself and one for Autocar in time for the coming summer season and also as in 1930, some service buses on Regal chassis were ordered for each company at the same time. These were

basically of the LGOC T-type design in its new form with front entrance but were 27ft long, the extra length being gained by the addition of a short bay at the rear. The bodies for Autocar were ordered from Park Royal who kept faithfully to the LGOC design. It appears that the original plan was for Autocar to have eight coaches, KR9911-8 and three buses, KR9919-21, but this was changed, possibly while the chassis were at Park Royal, so that KR9921 was completed as a coach and not a bus. The ESTC ordered three buses for themselves at the same time, but the bodies for these were contracted to Weymanns and are described below under T380-382.

T346-351, first licensed in March-April 1930, were ex-Blue Belle coaches with 26ft long bodies by London Lorries with rear swing doors. T352-357, first licensed in January-February 1931, were ex-Queen Line coaches also with London Lorries bodies but of improved design with rear sliding doors, although still only 26ft long. All 12 of these vehicles after being brought to a common 1931 chassis specification were fitted with new Weymann bodies of Chiswick design in October-November 1935. These bodies, 15121-15132, were similar in design to the 31 bodies for Reliances which they immediately followed but they differed from the latter in having the new tubular

aluminium seats. As first built only 26 seats were fitted. These vehicles were reclassified as buses in 1936 and the seating capacity was increased to 30 in 1938-39. They were coded 5T4 on rebodying. They were mostly, if not all, converted to run on producer gas during the war (code 13T4/1) but had all been converted back to petrol before its conclusion, when they were sold to the Allied Control Commission for use in Germany.

T358, first licensed in April 1930, had a rear entrance coach body with rear sliding door, said to be by a builder named Metcalfe. Was this, one wonders, the Metcalfe Engineering

Company of Romford whose premises served as one of the stabling points of the Green Line coaches when they were first introduced? T358 was sold in July 1938.

T360 and 363, licensed in June 1930, had 27ft long 31-seat Harrington half-canopy folding-roof coach bodies with two swing doors. They were used by the LPTB for private hire and sightseeing tours until the arrival of the LTC-type; they were sold in May 1938. T367 and 368, first licensed in May 1932, had later-type 27ft long Harrington sliding-roof 32-seat coach bodies with full-width canopies and rear sliding doors. After use on the Green Line services, T367

Left:
T370, ex-St Albans & District, with its original secondhand body, working from Hertford in LPTB days. *J. F. Higham*

Below:
T382, one of three buses built for the ESTC in 1931 with 27ft long front entrance Weymann bodies, working from Luton in LPTB days. *D. W. K. Jones*

was used on Central Area private hire and sightseeing tours in 1938 and sold in 1939; T368 may well have been intended for similar use during the summer of 1938, but it was sold in May.

The ex-Amersham coaches T359, 361, 362 and 364, first licensed respectively in December, October, October and April 1931, had 27ft long Strachan 32-seat coach bodies with rear sliding doors. They originally had luggage carriers on the roof which were removed in LPTB days; of 1931 chassis specification, they were coded 1/8T8/3 by the LPTB until they were converted to 11T11

in November 1938. T365 and 366, first licensed in May 1932, also had Strachan bodies incorporating some minor refinements. All six ex-Amersham coaches were used on the Green Line until the 1938 summer season when, following the disposal of most of the TR-type Leyland Tigers, they were used for private hire and sightseeing tours in the Central Area for which their sliding roofs made them suitable. After some indecision as to whether to convert T365 and 366 to 11T11 they were sold early in 1939.

All the foregoing vehicles which came to the LPTB were classified as coaches and were given the suffix C in 1935. T369-390 which all had doorless bodies were given the suffix B, as also were the ex-LGOC buses T15, 21, 25, 26 and 35.

T369 is a candidate for the bus with the most interesting history in this book. The chassis was originally built by AEC for demonstration in Lima, Peru. For this purpose it was fitted with a body numbered 11536 built by the LGOC at Chiswick in October 1930. This body was of the basic design used for T1-50 but had a rear open platform on the right-hand side, a round-fronted cab with a door, full-drop windows and a single line destination box. It was brought back to Britain in 1932 when the platform was reversed (possibly by Park Royal) and then sold to the Watford Omnibus Co by whom it was licensed in July of that year. It was in this condition when taken over by London Transport, by whom it was coded 4/1T6. However, in 1939 it was given a downgraded coach body from T300, whereupon it was recoded 1/7T7/1; in this form it survived until December 1949. This company's other Regal, T371, was an ex-AEC demonstration bus first licensed in March 1930 with a front-entrance body, details of which suggest that it was built by Shorts. T370 was built by AEC as a stock

chassis for the 1932 coach season, but having apparently failed to find a buyer it was bought by St Albans & District the following year and, fitted with a second-hand rear entrance body, was first licensed in June 1933. It was fitted with the spare Tilling body by the LPTB in September 1936 but both chassis and body were scrapped in October 1939, although both were barely 7 years old.

The ex-East Surrey buses T372-379 and T382-390 which had Hall Lewis rear-platform bodies of LGOC T-type design were first licensed in March 1930. T390 and 375-379 were orginally LGOC-owned and had LGOC body numbers (11135-40). T380-382, which had 27ft long front-entrance Weymann composite bodies with central rear emergency doors, were first licensed in May and June 1931. They appear on an LGOC sanction (24/1089) and had LGOC body numbers (13055, 13084/6). These three bodies seem to have been the first contract to have been placed with Weymann by the ESTC. Their design was basically a 27ft long front entrance version of the LGOC T-type body but unlike the two contemporary buses for Autocar bodied by Park Royal, the Weymann bodies on these three buses incorporated several departures from Chiswick detail. The chassis of T380, 662716, should have been T220, and a note on the card of the latter recorded the change as having been agreed with the ESTC — a matter imperfectly understood by the author and rather surprising, as the AEC sales note stipulated a frame length to suit 27ft body whereas T207-306 were 26ft long.

T370-390, along with the ex-LGOC buses T15, 21, 25, 26 and 35, were all delicensed in 1939. Some were sold later that year and others scrapped; all those which were still in stock in May 1945 were then sold to the Allied Control Commission for use in Europe.

Above:
Old Amersham garage as taken over from the Amersham & District Bus Co, whose name still appears on the fascia board although the vehicles have been repainted and lettered General. Those seen here include two ex-Amersham Regals, T359 and 366, and a Bluebird ST.
LT U14460

What are usually known as the Tilling T-type buses, T307-318, although operated by Tillings and fitted with Tilling bodies were in fact owned by the LGOC. They were bought in 1932 as replacements for older buses provided under an agreement between the two companies. They were covered by LGOC sanction 24/1143; a spare body was later added under sanction 24/1158. Despite the LGOC ownership of these buses the bodies did not receive Chiswick body numbers until after the Tilling business was taken over by the LPTB when they were numbered 13834-13846. T307-318 were first licensed in September 1932. The chassis were noteworthy for having as first built a special version of the six-cylinder petrol engine with a bore of only 95mm; these were replaced by standard 100mm bore engines at first overhaul, with which an axle ratio of 5.75:1 was used. T307 and 308 were originally fitted with Daimler gearboxes and AEC ball type selectors but these were removed on overhaul in 1934, in May and September respectively, and transferred into LT-type double-deckers. All 12 chassis had Lockheed hydraulic brakes.

The 26ft long bodies were of a seven-bay design with a doorless front entrance and rear emergency door, seating 30. The pillar spacing and windows were therefore common to the contemporary Tilling STLs, covered by the same sanction, which were of the same length. The LPTB codes were 3T3 for the buses with crash gearboxes and 4T3 for the two with fluid transmission; the bodies were provided with floor traps to suit either transmission. In 1936, as mentioned above, the body which was then spare was used for T370.

In later life these buses were much less restricted in their allocations than the former Tilling double-deck types; one reason for this was that they were adapted early in London Transport days to take standard single-deck destination blinds which made them interchangeable with the General T-type buses. Although none were ever converted to oil they lasted until the early 1950s.

London Transport inherited one AEC Renown, LT1429, from an independent operator, Hillmans of Romford. This was a long-wheelbase model of 1932 vintage with a Harrington half canopy luxury coach body which, despite its 30ft length, seated only 32. To make room for the sliding door the coachbuilders moved both fuel tanks to the offside. LT1429, which was petrol-engined with crash gearbox and triple servo brakes, was used by the LPTB for private hire. Coded 3LTL4, it perished in the air raid at Bull Yard in October 1940.

8: The Q and STL Types, 1932-34

From the beginning of 1932 the overall length limit for two-axle double-deckers was raised from 25ft to 26ft and the gross weight limit for two-axle vehicles from 9½ to 10 tons. To take advantage of these relaxations AEC increased the wheelbase of the Regent chassis to 16ft 3in.

The LGOC did not place orders for the longer wheelbase Regent immediately. They had just ordered the 250 60-seater Bluebirds, the introduction of which only began in February 1932, continued through the summer and was followed by the 23 ST-type Bluebirds for LGCS and the 22 special LT-type buses LT1405-1426 in the autumn.

Thus it was that the first 16ft 3in Regents to enter service in London were six buses bought by two independents, C. H. Pickup of Dulwich and E. Brickwood (Redline) of North Kensington. Both of these businesses were taken over by London Transport in November 1933. The five Pickup buses, which became STL553-557, are famous for having been built with open top decks — the last such buses to be built for service in London. Even so the bodies, which were built by Park Royal, had inside staircases and in this respect were more up to date than the City Omnibus Co's three Leyland Titanics built in 1933. STL553-6, which were on chassis which may have been built speculatively to offer quick delivery on potential sales at the Olympia Commercial Motor Show in November 1931, had triple servo brakes and received the LPTB code 12STL8, but STL557 had Lockheed hydraulic brakes and was distinguished by the LPTB code 1/12STL8. All five buses had petrol engines and crash gearboxes.

After being operated by London Transport for some months in their original form these buses were fitted with new top decks at Chiswick in May and June 1934. These were of the design then current for the STL3-type body, modified to suit the plan shape of the Park Royal body at first floor level. As the Park Royal body had six bays between lower saloon bulkheads whereas the Chiswick top deck had only five bays the appearance of these buses as rebuilt was very distinctive. In LPTB days they were allocated to the Tilling garages at Catford, Croydon and Bromley; STL554 was des-

Below:
Drama in the Old Kent Road, 23 October 1933. Pickup's open-top AEC Regent, soon to become STL553 in the LPTB fleet, is not yet two years old.
N. Baldwin Collection

troyed in the air raid on Croydon in May
1941. However, the other four buses lasted
until 1948-49; STL553 was given a late
standard STL body towards the end of its
life with which the semi-floating rear axle
looked rather incongruous. The last to
survive with its original body, STL556, spent
some time with the special events fleet after
withdrawal from regular service at Croydon
in April 1949.

STL558 was an even more interesting
bus. The chassis, which had Daimler
transmission with pedestal type selector
and triple-servo brakes, was delivered to
Brickwoods late in December 1931. It was
sent to Birch Bros in Kentish Town together
with a Daimler CF6 double-decker with an
outside staircase body which Birch Bros had
built two years earlier. The body was
removed from the Daimler chassis, which
was also of 16ft 3in wheelbase although
only 25ft long, extended and rebuilt at the
rear with an inside staircase and remounted
on the new AEC chassis. The CF6 chassis
was then sold.

When London Transport took over the
Brickwood business in November 1933,
STL558 and Brickwood's other modern bus,
the Daimler CH6 DST5, were both allocated
to Harrow Weald. Early the following year,
reportedly following an accident in Harrow
Weald garage in which it sustained rear-end

damage, STL558 was rebuilt at Chiswick
with an outside staircase of characteristically NS appearance, fitted with route
boards and a route number stencil front and
rear in place of the previous blinds and
repainted with the fleet name General which
was then still in use. Similar route boards
and stencils were fitted to the ex-
independent ST1028-1031, which also had
outside staircases and a central half-drop
window at the front through which they
could be changed. This was at a time when
Chiswick works was overwhelmed with
work resulting from the takeover of
independent undertakings and probably
could not keep up with the supply of blinds
in all the shapes and sizes required.

STL558, still with board and stencil
displays, was later moved to Catford. At
overhaul in 1939, however, it was fitted with
new roller blind destination boxes although
the full-drop windows were retained.
STL558 last worked in service in about 1943.
After a period of use for driver training, it
was sold early in 1946. I always thought it
was a mistake that it was not given a new
Chiswick petrol-STL body in 1934, when the
brake equipment might usefully have been
exchanged with STL557 and the pedestal-
type selector with one of the two ex-Tilling
T-type buses which were shortly to lose
their fluid transmission to Plumstead LTs.

Had these things been done, STL558 might have received an oil engine in 1939 and have survived in service into postwar days. It could even be said that fate had tried to push events in this direction as four spare bodies instead of the usual three were included in the sanction for STL353-452 which were being built at the time STL558 was in the works. Its LPTB code was 13STL9.

The decision to distinguish the 16ft 3in wheelbase version of the Regent as a new type with the letters STL does not appear to have been reached immediately by the LGOC, as the first order placed for 16ft 3in wheelbase Regent chassis was for 102 to replace the same number of LGOC-owned double-deckers operated by Thomas Tilling Ltd and when the first of these buses was completed at the beginning of October 1932 it was photographed with the number ST837 on its dumb-irons. STL1, the first LGOC bus, did not appear until January 1933, although STL1-50 had earlier chassis numbers than STL51-130, as the 80 Tilling buses which were actually delivered were now numbered. The last 22, which would have become STL131-152, were cancelled on the passing of the London Passenger Transport Act and these numbers always remained vacant. It is just conceivable that the number of buses cancelled — 22 — had some connection with the final LGOC order

for 22 LT-type chassis, but in any event 80 proved to be the number of bodies which Tilling was able to build before the LPTB came into being on 1 July 1933.

The sanction for the LGOC-owned buses operated by Tilling, 24/1143, covered the 12 Regal single-deckers which we met in the last chapter as well as the 102 double-deckers, these being the exact numbers of each type requiring replacement. The double-deck buses also had bodies designed and built by Tillings. These had inside stairs and 56 tubular-framed seats, but they were of typical Tilling appearance with three windows across the front of the upper deck, six-bay construction (this meant that the pillar spacing was the same as in the single-deck bodies) and small mean-looking destination blinds. The chassis all had 100mm bore petrol engines, crash gearboxes and Lockheed brakes. The last five or six had fully-floating axles as delivered but all 80 buses were coded 8STL4 by the LPTB. There were four spare bodies, built against LGOC sanction 24/1158, which must have come in useful after the air raid at Croydon garage in May 1941 when 22 of the Tilling STLs were destroyed. The others all survived the war. In 1948 some were transferred to Country Area and painted green. Two, STL59 and 75, received late standard Chiswick bodies. Although built

Above:
Redline's AEC Regent, the future STL558, in its original condition with 1930 Birch Bros body converted to inside staircase.
J. F. Higham

against LGOC sanctions the Tilling bodies did not receive Chiswick body numbers until after the Tilling business was taken over by London Transport, when they were numbered 14042-14125.

The design of the bodies produced at Chiswick for the first 50 General STLs (sanction 24/1150, body Nos 13470-13519), which began to appear in January 1933, was much more ambitious. It had a seating capacity of 60. To achieve this the top deck was carried right forward to overhang the radiator and as a five-bay construction was adopted this did not look too outrageous. The body was decidedly austere, lacking the moulded waistrails of the LT and ST-type bodies and single-panelled throughout. These sacrifices were necessary to achieve the unladen weight target of 6 tons and in fact the licensing weight came out at 5T18C, an achievement which the lightweight seats made possible. The springs had to be rather hard to meet the tilt test with 34 seats on the upper deck and possibly for the same reason the destination gear was rearranged in the upper deck panelling, three boxes now being used front and rear. The appearance of the General STL was uncompromisingly functional, lacking the elegance achieved with the Bluebird design. One consequence of its being designed to the limits imposed by the length and weight constraints, was that all the first 50 buses had petrol engines and all but one had crash gearboxes. The engines were of 100mm bore with which an axle ratio of 6.25:1 was used. Twenty of the 50 buses were delivered with fully floating axles of the new AEC design and all had Lockheed brakes. These had now become standard and the

hydraulic master cylinder was combined with the vacuum servo.

The one exception to the standard specification was STL50. This had a Daimler preselective gearbox with a pedestal type selector which were fitted before the chassis was delivered from AEC in April 1933. As AEC had used the ball-type selector since the previous summer the inference is that the transmission equipment was not then new and my guess is that it was the set originally fitted to ST746. STL50 as delivered had no fluid flywheel; in this respect it was like the early Armstrong Siddeley cars mentioned in Chapter 5. The reason for dispensing with the fluid flywheel was, undoubtedly, that trouble was being experienced with petrol-engined buses with fluid transmission stalling when being asked to idle in gear. Presumably AEC were involved both in making the special driveline parts required and establishing the best settings of the gearbox bands to give an acceptable take-off. This equipment not having been specified in the sanction, STL 50 did not receive any proper LPTB code. It was given the makeshift code 3STL1, but the chassis was not identical with STL203-252 (to which the chassis code 3STL belonged) and the body was unique in the batch built for STL1-50 in having a floor trap for a midships gearbox.

STL1-50 were all sent to Clay Hall when new, but STL50 was shortly moved to Plumstead. It was fitted with a fluid flywheel in 1934. In postwar years when I knew it, it was at Potters Bar, where it was mainly used for driver training. It was on such a duty when brought into Chiswick one day during the time I was there in 1946 when I noticed that it had a pedestal-type selector. This, like the one in STL558, could usefully have been exchanged with the ball type selectors originally fitted in T307 and 308 when their Daimler gearboxes were transferred into LT-type buses in 1934.

STL1-50 were followed by STL153-202 which were further buses with bodies of the same design. These however had coil ignition and a different exhaust layout and type of silencer, and were coded 2STL1 whereas STL1-49 were coded 1STL1. STL153-202 shared sanction 24/1159 with STL203-252, all of which had Daimler gearboxes without, originally, fluid flywheels. These buses had ball type selectors. With them a reversion was made to 56-seat bodies, of an unattractive and undistinguished sloping front design. The sanction included four spare bodies (the body numbers being 13547-13650) three of which were of the 60-seater type.

Before either of these types appeared the LGOC had licensed a strikingly unconventional single-decker, Q1, which was placed in service experimentally on route 11 from Hammersmith on 5 September 1932. Q1 was the first example of the AEC Q-type chassis, the original concept of which was

entirely Rackham's. Rackham not only designed the chassis but had a model made to show both bodybuilder and customer what the finished vehicle should look like. In its single-deck form the Q-type was 27ft 6in long with a wheelbase of 18ft 6in, for use with a central entrance (a later version had a shorter wheelbase to allow a front entrance) and Q1 would have been noteworthy if for no other reason as the first 27ft 6in long two axle bus to run in London. The concept placed a wheel close to each corner and single wheels were used front and rear with 10.50×20 tyres, four of which would have supported an evenly distributed gross weight of 9 tons. The engine was placed outside the frame behind the offside front wheel, or more exactly the radiator occupied this position with the engine immediately behind it. The entire driveline was outside the frame as far as the rear axle, where the frame splayed outwards and the propeller shaft passed under the spring to a worm drive differential just inboard; the use of single wheels allowed the differential to be offset to a considerably greater extent than it could have been with twins. The most surprising feature of all, and I cannot explain the reason for it even today, was the

Below:
Ex-Tilling STL80 at Marble Arch, May 1935. *LT U17308*

adoption of anticlockwise engine rotation. Whatever the reason was, there is no doubt that this feature complicated the Q-type as a product by necessitating a special starter, oil pump, worm and wheel and (later) gearbox, to mention just a few components.

As well as the anticlock rotation the engine was special in having all the manifolding on the offside and also in the block being inclined outwards at 15° to the vertical. In most respects it was a handed version of the 110mm bore petrol engine and as produced for the LGOC, employing what was known as the standard head, was given the unit number A167. Subsequent petrol engines used the new AEC high power head and these were A169. The axle ratio used in the single-decker was 5.2:1. The axle itself was of a new design with fully-floating shafts and accommodated an 8in centres worm drive differential.

The first chassis was built as a joint project between AEC and the LGOC. It had a crash gearbox transmission, mounted as a unit with the engine. Experience with this convinced Rackham that all future Q-type chassis should have fluid transmission, even though, because of the anticlockwise engine rotation, this meant producing a special gearbox.

There is some doubt whether Q1 had Lockheed brakes. The rolling stock card for this vehicle described it as having Dewandre brakes (Dewandre was the inventor of the vacuum servo used with both systems) whereas the cards for all subsequent Q-type buses referred to Lockheed brakes. At the time the design was prepared, early in 1932, chassis-mounted triple servo brakes were still standard for orthodox chassis with crash transmission. The note on the card is thus inconclusive, although Lockheed brakes then being new, one would have expected them to have been mentioned if fitted.

Having the gearbox, engine, radiator and driving position all on the offside produced a concentration of weight on that side which could not be fully balanced by positioning the fuel tank and batteries on the nearside. As a result the centre of gravity was displaced from the longitudinal centre line and the Q-type had to have different springs offside and nearside on both axles (as the Regal Mark IV had to have 18 years later).

This was a matter of more importance when it came to the double-deck version which Rackham designed next. Here again he had a model made and in this case AEC also had the first chassis bodied as a demonstrator. This body was built by Metro-Cammell to an outline design prepared by Rackham. Interestingly, AEC photographs show that it had seats closely derived from the LGOC round-backed design in vogue during the second half of 1931 which would have been specified for the 25 Dennis Lances for which Metro-Cammell built the bodies. In this respect it was unlike Q1 which had seats of the type

Left:
STL1, posed photograph at Chiswick, January 1933.
LT U11679

89

introduced with the Bluebirds, as did the later Q2 and 3.

The double-decker was, if anything, more strikingly unconventional in appearance than the single-decker. The overall length was, naturally, reduced to the permitted limit of 26ft but the wheelbase was reduced proportionately more, to 15ft 10in so that although the rear wheels were still close to the rear corners of the vehicle the front overhang was considerably greater and accommodated the entrance. The proportions of the vehicle were thus exactly reversed compared with what was accepted as orthodox at the time. Although this was still 25 years in the future, the layout would have permitted one-man-operation, but even with the entrance in this position there was no door. The double-decker ran on 11.25 × 20 tyres, a size larger than the single-decker, to support the permitted maximum gross weight of 10 tons. The demonstration prototype, which had seats for 60 passengers and weighed just over 6 tons, had enough margin in hand to allow it to be converted to an oil engine (of a new type specially designed for the Q-type, unit number A170) when this became available early in 1934. Records show that it visited Chiswick from 27 September to 5 October 1932. At this stage it was petrol-engined; it might have improved its chances of winning a worthwhile order from the LGOC if it had been fitted with a diesel engine, but in the event no orders were placed until just after the formation of the LPTB, when two buses, Q2 and 3, were ordered for Central Area and two for Country Area.

The AEC demonstration prototype, chassis number 761001, seems to have been built with the possibility of eventual sale to Birmingham in mind* as it had not only a Daimler preselective gearbox but a right-hand quadrant control. As briefly mentioned above, the gearbox had to be of a special design because of the anticlockwise rotation of the engine and Wilson prevailed upon Daimler to produce a special version of their gearbox, AEC unit number D129. Daimler gearboxes of this type were fitted to the double-deck prototype and all subsequent Q-type chassis produced during 1933. These included 11 double-deckers, the last two of which, chassis numbers 761011 and 012, were London Transport's Q2 and 3. These and probably all of the others were petrol-engined. For both petrol and oil-engined models the axle ratio used was 6.2:1.

The body which the LGOC designed and built for Q1 followed the AEC wooden model fairly closely, even to the extent of originally having a black roof and upper parts which were totally foreign to LGOC ideas of vehicle livery. The departures which were made, in respect of headlamp position, pillar spacing and the shape of the rear dome, were all for the worse as far as appearance was concerned.

Q1 did not remain long at Hammersmith. On 28 October it was moved to Nunhead which had a single-deck route on which it

* After running as a demonstrator in Birmingham for most of 1933, this vehicle returned to Southall at the end of the year or possibly early in 1934. It was then fitted with an oil engine, probably the second such engine produced, before returning to Birmingham, by whom it was bought and added to stock as BCT No 93.

could be used. Having originally been built as a joint venture with AEC, it became LGOC property on 1 January 1933 when it was covered by sanction 24/1154 and received body number 13466. On 4 December following it was lent by the LPTB to Country Area for trial on the Green Line. It cannot have been ideal for such use as the seats were of the lightweight wooden-framed type fitted to the Bluebirds and five of these on the offside were longitudinal. It was permanently transferred to Country Area on 13 February 1934 when it was once again classified as a bus. It remained at Reigate until 30 September 1942 when it was delicensed. After being stored at Tunbridge Wells and Guildford it was sold in January 1946.

Q2 and 3 were ordered on London Transport Sanction D10, which was actually the first order for buses for Central Area placed by the new authority. The chassis were delivered in November 1933 and sent for bodying to Metropolitan-Cammell at Saltley who, in fact, built the bodies for most of the customers for the Q-type double-deckers who accepted the front entrance concept. Although the Metro-Cammell design adhered closely to the AEC model, the London Transport vehicles had the very comprehensive destination display used in contemporary STL-type buses and this made them particularly handsome and imposing vehicles. However, the completed buses were not delivered to Chiswick until late in May 1934. With 55 seats they weighed 6T4C2Q. They were licensed early

in July and allocated to Harrow Weald after being photographed at Chiswick wearing Chalk Farm plates.

On 29 May 1937, Q2 and 3 were transferred to Country Area in exchange for ST819 and 820. After initially being at Leatherhead they were moved to Hertford in July 1938 where they remained until July 1939. They were then moved to Grays, only to be delicensed on 30 September following the outbreak of war. During the war Q2 and 3 were stored at various locations and while serving as a mobile Home Guard command post at Swanley Junction in June 1941 Q3 was destroyed by enemy action. In company with Q4, 5 and 188, Q2 was moved to Walthamstow (Forest Road Works) in January 1944 and sold in March 1946.

The first two orders for buses for Country Area sanctioned by the London Passenger Transport Board were two Q-type double-deckers (sanction E1) ostensibly for the Green Line services and 12 Regent double-deckers (sanction E2) with low-height front entrance bodies to replace the remaining PS-type open-top vehicles at Godstone used on Route 410. At this stage Country Area was administered from Reigate, still being effectively the London General Country Services organisation, and consequently all 14 buses received Surrey registrations. These buses were not numbered until the administration of country buses was transferred to Chiswick on 25 February 1935; they then received the numbers Q4 and 5 and STL1044-1055, and respective codes 3Q3 and 11STL7. They also then received LPTB body numbers.

Left:
Q2 after its transfer to Country Area, working from Hertford in 1938. *J. F. Higham*

In terms of chassis specification, the two Q-types and the Regents make an interesting contrast. Q4 and 5 were petrol-engined and had fluid transmission, although unlike Q2 and 3 their gearboxes were of AEC manufacture (unit number D133). STL1044-1055, however, were fitted with 8.8-litre AEC-Ricardo oil engines, type A165, and had crash gearboxes. It must be remembered that the A165 unit was the only oil engine available from AEC at the time these buses were ordered. Had they been ordered a year later, the two Q-types would very likely have had the A170 oil engine and the Regents the A171 with much commonality of parts. In 1933, the only experience the Country Services had had of oil engines was with the A161-type AEC-Ricardo engines in the three coaches T216, 274 and 305 transferred with the Green Line operation on 29 July 1932.

Q4 and 5 and the 12 Regents all had Lockheed brakes, these being standard on AEC passenger chassis in 1933. They also had Weymann bodies (built at Addlestone in Surrey, in the heart of LGCS territory) which has some notable similarities despite the differences in chassis type and overall height. The similarities included irregular pillar spacing (associated with the entrance and staircase positions), an elliptical arch over the passenger doorway, a central rear emergency door, sidelights at upper deck floor level, three destination boxes front and rear and one above the entrance doorway. In Q4 and 5 the latter and the staircase were amidships, with a pair of sliding doors which were electropneumatically operated. In the Regents the entrance was at the front of the saloon with a single sliding door, which was manually operated, and the staircase was placed transversely against the front bulkhead. In both designs the route

number was masked behind the glass in a full-depth aperture, a feature which had not yet been adopted in STL bodies built at Chiswick, or indeed in Q2 and 3.

If after delivery in May 1934 (earlier than Q2 or 3) Q4 and 5 were tried on the Green Line service at Reigate, it was not long before they were reclassified as country buses. They were teamed with Q2 and 3 at Leatherhead in 1937, at Hertford in 1938 (where they were joined by Q188) and at Grays in 1939. Their subsequent history is also similar up to their being sold in March 1946. With Q188, Q4 and 5 later saw service with Gareloch Motor Services of Garelochhead, Scotland.

Delivered in April and May 1934, STL1044-1055 spent most of their lives at Godstone working the Reigate-Bromley route for which they were bought. The 8.8-litre engines were converted to direct injection during the war in common with the A165 engines fitted in Central Area LT-type buses.

Although the formal order for STL1044-1055 was not placed until after the formation of the LPTB in July 1933, their chassis numbers fell between the Tilling and second General series. Like the latter they all had fully floating rear axles. When STL1044-1055 were replaced at Godstone by new buses in 1950 the bodies were found to be so sound that all 12 buses saw another two years' service at Guildford and Addlestone.

The change over to the new regime on 1 July 1933 found Chiswick building 56-seat double-deckers on 16ft 3in wheelbase Regent chassis. These buses, STL203-252, had 100mm bore petrol engines, Daimler D128 gearboxes with AEC ball-type selectors but without fluid flywheels, fully floating rear axles with 6.25:1 ratio and

Right:
Q5 working from Leatherhead at Kingston in 1936. *J. F. Higham*

Lockheed brakes with the master cylinder combined with the servo. The LPTB code for these buses was 3STL2 or 1/3STL2, the latter denoting a minor engine modification.

The next sanction, 24/1169, covering 100 buses numbered STL253-352, was the last order for buses by the LGOC. It included 50 with crash and 50 with Daimler preselective gearboxes of which 11 were to have oil engines of a new type, unit number A171. These 11 buses had fluid flywheels, which the petrol-engined preselective buses originally did not. Included in the contract were 89 oil engines intended for LT-type buses, these being of the A165 (8.8-litre) type. Consequently the engines fitted in STL253-341 when they entered service were of the A145-type (110mm bore with standard head) with which an axle ratio of 5.75:1 was used. These engines had been removed from LT-type buses which it was intended to convert to oil and were supplied free issue to AEC after reconditioning at Chiswick. The codes allocated to these buses were as follows:

STL253-291 (petrol engine and Daimler preselective gearbox): 4STL3/2
STL292-341 (petrol engine and crash gearbox): 6STL3
STL342-352 (A171 oil engine, fluid flywheel, Daimler gearbox): 5STL3/1

By the middle of 1933, AEC had designed an oil engine for the Q-type. Naturally this has to be completely special in having anticlock rotation and all the auxiliaries on the offside. With a considerable body of experience to draw upon, AEC was now confidently able to design the new engine so that it was no longer than the petrol engine; the Q-type petrol engine used the same crankshaft as the petrol engines used in the orthodox chassis, and there was much commonality of other parts. The oil engine was based on the same cylinder centres and used the Ricardo Comet Combustion system from the start. With a bore of 106mm and a stroke of 146mm, the swept volume was 7.74 litres and the rated power 115bhp at 2,000rpm. The crankshaft had big end and main bearings of 68mm and 75mm diameter respectively and these ran in lead bronze. The camshaft was located in the cylinder block, allowing two cylinder heads to be used whilst making the pushrods as short as possible.

The A171 was an orthodox version of the A170 Q-type oil engine, with the auxiliaries on the nearside. It shared all the specification details mentioned above and the only clue to its origin was the firing order 1-4-2-6-3-5, compared with the more usual 1-5-3-6-2-4. The engines fitted in STL342-352 were, with the spare supplied, probably the first 12 such engines produced. Happily they were completely successful and were destined to power more than 2,000 London Transport buses built between 1934 and 1938.

The Daimler gearboxes supplied for STL342-352 were of modified type incorporating a dynamo drive as mentioned in Chapter 5. In the event the last three buses were delivered with gearboxes of the new AEC D132-type and the displaced Daimler gearboxes were fitted to STL403-405 of the next sanction. On a contemporary LPTB data sheet, however, STL342-352 are shown as having Daimler gearboxes and it is likely that these gearboxes were later exchanged to bring them into line with the data sheet. The 103 bodies built for STL252-352, 13685-13786, were a slightly improved

Right:
Godstone STL1052 showing its passenger door seen on a wet day in Reigate in 1937.
N. Baldwin Collection

Below:
STL203, the first of the LGOC 56-seat design, posed for the photographer at Chiswick, July 1933. The only visible clue to the new ownership is the absence of the LGOC transfer. *LT H14145*

version of the STL2 design, still with the same seats and trim but with a neater and less angular arrangement of the front windows.

The next sanction for 100 buses, STL353-452, was the first order for STL-type buses to be placed by the LPTB (sanction D11, with 104 bodies 14156-14259). With it or at about the same time AEC were notified of the Board's intention to standardise on the Wilson gearbox transmission. This was the signal AEC was waiting for to negotiate its own licence to build this gearbox. This order again included 50 buses with crash and 50 with preselective gearboxes, the former being STL353-402 and the latter STL403-452, codes 6STL3 and 7STL3/2 respectively. All were fitted with 110mm bore reconditioned petrol engines removed from LT chassis for which A165 oil engines were again supplied loose. With STL403-452 fluid flywheels were again specified and at the same time (this was early in 1934) London Transport began refitting them to the earlier buses (STL50 and 203-291) which had been delivered without them. The AEC preselective gearbox, unit number D132 (the Q-type version was D133), was very similar to the D128 unit which Wilson had designed for Daimler. The principal difference was the use of wider ratios (4.50, 2.53, 1.64 and 1.00:1 with 6.9:1 reverse).

STL453-552, which formed the next sanction (D15, with 103 bodies 14356-14458), were all fitted with fluid flywheels, D132 gearboxes and 110mm bore ex-LT reconditioned petrol engines, a similar number of A165 oil engines for LTs again being supplied loose. The STL3/2 bodies for this batch were improved in detail without being altered in outline; the most noticeable changes were the adoption of a full depth glass for the route number aperture and the use of a thin aluminium beading round the lower panels instead of a thick wooden one.

The next sanction (D26) was for 200 buses of which the first 50, STL559-608, were a repeat of STL453-552, and again 50 8.8-litre oil engines were supplied loose for use in LT-type buses. Although included in the same order, STL609-758 marked the beginning of a new era, that of the London Transport standard double-decker for the next five years, whereas STL559-608 were the last buses built to a pure LGOC design. The sanction for STL559-758 included 206 bodies, 14492-14697, of which the first 51 were of the STL3/2- type.

The later history of the petrol STLs included several features of interest. When in 1934 fluid flywheels were fitted to all the buses originally built without them (STL50 and 203-291) an exception was made of STL221, which was chosen in March of that year for an experimental installation of the Leyland-Lysholm-Smith torque converter transmission. The success of the Daimler fluid flywheel transmission had naturally obliged Leyland to offer a more advanced alternative to the friction clutch and crash gearbox on its bus models and the alternative which Leyland chose was the Lysholm-Smith three-stage torque converter.

The original concept of the hydrokinetic torque converter was invented by Dr Fottinger who also invented the fluid coupling which we have already met. A torque converter resembles a fluid coupling in that the drive is transmitted from an input member to an output member by the momentum of oil circulating in a toroidal path, but it differs in that the blades are curved and in having a third member in the circuit, called the reaction member, which is grounded to the casing. When the speed of the output member is appreciably less than that of the input member, the circulation of oil over the curved blades of the reaction member develops a reaction torque upon it (whence its name). The output torque, which is the sum of the input torque and the reaction torque, is then greater than the input torque from the engine, and so the torque converter resembles a gearbox. The design adopted by Leyland was of three-stage type, in which after leaving the impeller or input member the oil passed alternately over three sets of output blades and reaction blades before it got back to the impeller. With this design the output torque at standstill was five times input torque, rather more than first gear in a typical bus gearbox. The efficiency was then zero, but as the bus got under way it rose rapidly so that by the time a condition corresponding to second gear was reached it was over 50%, and in that corresponding to third gear it was 80% or more. Above this there was a difficulty in that the efficiency began to fall again but this was circumvented in the Leyland design by incorporating a two-way friction clutch, operated by the driver with a hand lever, which cut out the drive through the torque converter and substituted a direct drive equivalent to top gear. Reversing apart, this was the only operation the driver had to perform. Reverse was obtained in a dog-clutch gearbox on the output side of the torque converter by sideways movement of the same lever. There was no pedal, and as the drive passed through no gears in forward motion the transmission could truthfully be called gearless. Leyland buses fitted with it proclaimed Leyland Gearless Bus on the radiator grille.

Although the Leyland Gearless transmission was made available to selected operators for trial in 1932 none of the Leyland buses taken over by London Transport was thus equipped. It is a little surprising that STL221 was chosen in preference to one of these, particularly as they included some recent model TD2 Titans and even some with oil engines. Refitted with its body in April, STL221 ran with its torque converter first at Clay Hall and later at Upton Park until August 1937. By that time the torque-converter equipped

STD91-100 were in service and STL221 was converted back to a Daimler gearbox transmission but with fluid flywheel. I have never seen fuel consumption figures for STL221, but with its torque converter and petrol engine they would probably have been about 4mpg.

In 1938 three buses previously equipped with Daimler gearboxes, STL253, 263 and 290, were fitted with experimental AEC synchromesh gearboxes. As the gearboxes were mounted amidships, clutch and gearbox were separated by a rubber-bushed drive shaft. Thus equipped these three buses were coded 1/4STL3/2. The synchromesh gearboxes were replaced with standard AEC crash gearboxes during the war, making these buses standard with STL292-341 and 353-402, code 6STL3. As a result of this exercise, they missed being converted to diesel in 1939 and with the other petrol-engined STLs were withdrawn in 1947-51.

All the petrol-engined buses with Chiswick 56-seat bodies and fluid transmission, whether with AEC or Daimler gearboxes, were converted to oil engines in 1939. The engines fitted were of the toroidal direct-injection type, AEC unit No A173, as fitted to the contemporary buses of the 15STL16-type. Like the latter, the converted buses were given rubber engine mountings — a change which must have added appreciably to the cost on conversion. After a change of plan, the original bodies were refitted with minimum alteration although with the chassis they were now recoded 16STL18 (STL403-552 and 559-608, with AEC gearboxes); 1/16STL18 (STL254-262, 264-289 and 292, with Daimler gearboxes), and 2/16STL18/1 (STL203-252, which also had Daimler gearboxes). The original ball type selectors fitted to all these buses were retained on conversion, working adequately well with the rubber-mounted engine.

Some body changes took place during the war; STL177 and 190 acquired 56-seat bodies of the STL3-type. Converted STL267 acquired an STL18/1-type body (of the type originally fitted to STL203-252); STL258 and 259 acquired 1941 wartime bodies of the STL17-type, with the same type of seats and mudwings as the originals but having the later standard STL outline; STL445, 548, 576 and 582 received bodies of types built for later standard oil-engined STL batches and petrol-engined STL384 acquired a 60-seater STL1-type body. STL342-352 and the oil-engined conversions were withdrawn between 1952 and 1954.

9: London Transport Standard Double-Deckers, 1934-39

When STL609 appeared in November 1934, it was at once apparent that its design represented a great step forward in terms of appearance. This was a result of deliberate policy on the part of London Transport to improve the visual impact of its artefacts seen by the public, including such things as stations, trains, buses, bus stop signs and notices. The changes to the STL body needed to achieve this transformation were relatively slight except at the front. Here a continuous curve from the cab dashboard to the roof cantrail replaced the previous step and slope, the effect, in side elevation, being to make the curve of the front match that of the rear. The increased length of the upper saloon at cantrail level was about 9in. The lower edges of the windscreen and also the front bulkhead windows were curved down to meet the waistrail of the saloon side windows while still clearing the bonnet, whose height was unaltered. On the offside the waistrail forward of the cab doorway (there was still no door) was now at the same height as that of the side windows. The happy addition of a valance extending from the inner screen pillar to the nearside front bulkhead pillar at the height of the top

of the windscreen and painted in the off-white of the window surrounds brought a much-needed relief to the front view. This came below the deep black band between the decks, which was retained; use was originally made of it to incorporate the side lights, but these had to be moved to the orthodox positions on cab front and bulkhead on the outbreak of war to conform with emergency lighting regulations. The bulkhead itself was cleaned up by moving the Autovac to a position within the bonnet.

At the rear the only changes were the addition of a prominent S-bend to the upper deck cantrail band behind the rearmost side window, bringing it down to waistrail level, and filling-in of most of the window space at the side of the staircase; where a full-size lower deck window had been incorporated in earlier STL bodies there was now only a small window and an area of plain panel. The platform and staircase were unaltered from previous STL bodies (and the Bluebirds in fact), the familiar arrangement with two single seats upstairs being retained. The central portion of the body was unaltered except for the addition of rearward sweeps behind the mudguards, front

Below:
STL813, a Merton example of the early LPTB standard STL, at Morden in March 1936. Merton had more than 200 of the first 350 standard STLs. ST1046, standing next to STL813, is on one of the through workings between Morden and Dorking transferred to the ESTC in April 1931 which continued to be worked by Country Area until 1938. It was actually one of the last two buses to be bought by the ESTC. *LT U19853*

and rear. Inside, a brighter effect was achieved by carrying the primrose colour of the ceilings on both decks halfway down the window pillars, but for all its improved appearance the STL5 body was still single-panelled and still had the lightweight wooden-framed seats introduced with the Bluebirds. The destination display was unchanged from the later STL3/2-type bodies.

STL609-758, coded 9STL, with 155 bodies (14543-14697) were the balance of sanction D26 which also covered STL559-608. They were powered by the new A171 7.7-litre AEC oil engine with Ricardo Comet Mk 1 heads as fitted to STL342-352. Transmission was by fluid flywheel and AEC D132 self-changing gearbox with ball type selector. The chassis-mounted 8in dynamo was chain driven from the front of the gearbox. The fuel tank remained on the offside, and the rear axle ratio was kept at 5.75:1.

The first examples of the 9STL5 buses were sent to Hanwell, the traditional trial ground for new types of oil engines, which had also received STL342-352. This suggests a certain timidity of approach by

London Transport; however, they were soon spread among the main Central Area garages, such as Dalston, Hackney and especially Merton, from which many of the principal cross-town routes were worked.

The pattern established with STL609-758 was followed with variations until 1939. Ultimately there were more than 2,000 buses which conformed to this basic formula. Just as the ST and LT-types had replaced the K and S-types the STL and STD-types were to replace the NS-type and various more recent double-deckers including the 173 early Titans of the TD-type, 33 Dennis Lances of the DL-type and the three ex-City Leyland Titanics.

Next followed a batch of 85 buses for Country Area, STL959-1043. Ordered on sanction E20 in August 1934, their chassis numbers immediately preceded the next 200 buses for Central Area which were presumably ordered at the same time or very shortly afterwards. Although the Country Area buses were built first, entering service between March and May 1935, they were numbered after STL759-958, which were completed between May and

November. STL959-1043 replaced all the Country Area double-deckers of the PS and NS-types and in fact all inherited double-deckers except those of the TD and ST-types.

The chassis of STL959-1043 were effectively of the same specification as the Central Area buses, with 7.7-litre Comet Mk 1 engines, fluid transmission and Lockheed brakes. In the undressed state they could be distinguished by a prominent bracket attached to each frame side-member close to the rear spring shackle. This last was an addition to support the rear part of the body, which was of front entrance layout although very similar in outline to the contemporary Central Area design.

In May 1934 Country Area had received the 12 Godstone buses with front entrances. These had made a very favourable impression on the operating management; they had, however, a sliding passenger door which the Chiswick design office regarded as an unnecessary complication for a stage carriage bus. To forestall complaints of draughts with previous front entrance layouts, in the Chiswick design both the bulkhead and the return between the step and the saloon were angled. This arrangement meant that the entrance occupied two whole bays of the body with the result that the foremost seat on the nearside had to be a single. As first built these bodies only had 19 seats on the lower deck because a luggage stand was provided over the wheel arch on either side. In 1939 these were each replaced by a double longitudinal seat increasing the lower deck seating capacity to 23. As in the Godstone design (and the 1933 trolleybus No 61) there was a central rear emergency door.

The upper deck seating capacity of 29 was only one less than that of the Central Area rear entrance body. The layout adopted used three single seats on the nearside opposite the staircase well, in front of which there was a triple. The original total of 48 seats was the same as the lowbridge Godstone buses, a peculiarity of which (and one which they retained throughout their lives) was that the seats on the upper deck were alternately in rows of three and four. In the Chiswick bodies the seats were of the contemporary hollow-backed plywood type introduced with the Bluebirds.

STL 959-1043 were coded 10STL6. The 85 bodies were numbered 14812-14896. The Godstone buses which had previously been unnumbered received the numbers STL 1044-1055 and the code 11STL7 when the Country Area engineering function was transferred to Chiswick on 25 February 1935. Four further 10STL6-type buses, STL1056-1059, which were completed in July 1935, must have been ordered very soon after this event; the sanction covering the purchase of these buses was H52, with body Nos 15512-15515.

At exactly the same time that responsibility for Country Area engineering and maintenance was transferred to Chiswick an event took place which led to a second order for four oil-engined Regent chassis being placed with AEC. This was the withdrawal from service of the four Daimler CH6 buses which London Transport had inherited, DST1, 2, 3, and 5. The first three of these were the LGOC buses we met in Chapter 5; these had ST2-type bodies and nearside fuel tanks. DST5 had come from E. Brickwood Ltd (Redline) of North Kensington; it had an inside-stair Dodson body and an offside fuel tank. The bodies were removed from all four

Above right:
STL857 as first built, while temporarily renumbered STF1, near Kensal Rise in 1936.
J. F. Higham Collection

Right:
STL1167 working from Camberwell Green in 1947 with the original body from STL857 after conversion to half cab.
Author

chassis in February 1935 and the chassis were sold the following month. After standing on trolleys at Chiswick for between 15 and 18 months the bodies were fitted to four special 15ft 6½in wheelbase chassis with nearside fuel tanks which had been ordered on sanction DA51 and delivered in December 1935, and as STL1260-1263 they entered service between May and September 1936. The last of the four to enter service was STL1262, which received the Dodson body from DST5. All the bodies were by this time more than five years old.

I have often wondered if STL1056-1059 were originally ordered for the purpose of carrying the four ex-DST bodies and only diverted to Country Area when it was realised that there was a difference which would make this impossible. However, I am now convinced that they were bought to meet a need arising from a route between Sevenoaks and Tonbridge formerly worked by Redcar Services Ltd which was taken over from Maidstone & District (which had acquired Redcar the previous February) on 31 July 1935. The chassis were delivered to Chiswick on 2 and 3 July and the completed buses were licensed on the 16th and 17th, two of them being sent to Dunton Green and the other two to Swanley. Country buses were usually ordered for *bona fide* Country Area purposes and in this case the chassis would have had the large bracket behind the rear axle which I have mentioned in connection with STL959-1043. However, I do not know at what stage this bracket was put on the chassis, and it was presumably removed from some of these chassis which were later fitted with rear entrance bodies. What is surprising is that four Leyland Titans, TD192-195, were taken over with the Redcar route, were moved to Windsor and survived until 1939. No comparable order for new vehicles was placed when the coach route between London and Tunbridge Wells formerly worked by Redcar was taken over at the same time, with six Leyland Tiger coaches.

Apart from the wheelbase, STL1260-1263 were of the contemporary standard specification having 7.7-litre Comet Mᴋ 1 oil engines, fluid transmission, Lockheed brakes and fully floating rear axles. When new they were allocated to Tottenham, but they were later moved to Cricklewood where they remained throughout the war working on Route 60. In 1944 the Dodson body on STL1262 which had been wrecked by a flying bomb was replaced by a standard ST2-type body on to which an STL-type cab was grafted. In 1947 the units were transferred into a standard 16ft 3in chassis frame with offside fuel tank and STL1262 received a standard 56-seat roof-indicator body. STL1260, 1261 and 1263 were transferred to Edgware shortly afterwards and were withdrawn in 1950 not long after the last of the ST-type. STL1262, which now bore a certain similarity to the celebrated axe in the Tower of London, lasted until 1952.

STL1260-1263 were coded 14STL10, without distinction for the Dodson body on STL1262. The whole episode can only be described as bizarre, especially when one remembers that without looking beyond Central Area there were obvious candidates for the Chiswick bodies in ST1028-1031. ST1028 in fact would probably have accepted a standard ST-type body without modification. The decision to specify near-side fuel tanks on STL1260-1263 must have caused inconvenience at garages throughout their lives as no other diesel-engined buses in the LPTB fleet had the fuel tank on this side until the advent of the RT-type. The chassis numbers of STL1260-1263 (06613715-8) were earlier than those of STL1060-1259 (06613793-3992), indicating that these four special chassis were ordered first, although possibly not at that time allocated their eventual bonnet numbers. Logically, they should have been numbered in the ST-type. The chassis were the only 15ft 6½in wheelbase Regents built after the LGCS Bluebirds in 1932 unless 6613719, a petrol-engined chassis bought for use as a service lorry, was another.

STL759-958 which were ordered on sanction DA41 were all in essential respects a repeat of ST609-758, with a very similar chassis specification but not quite identical as the licensing weight went up from 6T4C2Q to 6T6C0Q, possibly reflecting a change in engine crankcase material from magnesium to aluminium alloy. With the 15 exceptions referred to below, the 206 bodies built for this sanction (15133-15338) were originally intended to be coded STL5/1, but the differences from the previous batch were evidently so slight that it was decided to code them STL5. However, the last 15 bodies (15324-15338) which were built with seats of greatly improved design with tubular aluminium frames were coded STL5/2.

STL857 was chosen for considerably more extensive modifications involving mainly the body but also extending to equipment usually regarded as part of the chassis. It was built with a full-fronted body, generally based on the standard STL structure but with considerably greater frontal curvature and with some increase in rear curvature to match. The radiator was concealed behind a grille carried on the body and the bonnet was of a kind used on contemporary AEC goods chassis, as the cab was the full width of the body. However, instead of a cab door on the nearside there was an access door for engine maintenance below window level behind the front wheel. Although both side and front screens drooped towards the corner pillars the driving position had to be raised in an attempt to provide adequate nearside vision. It is likely that deficiencies in this respect plus a probable increase in cab noise level which led this experiment to be discontinued after about 18 months.

The modifications made to the body included the use of tubular aluminium seats as used in the STL5/2 type bodies, but it was also double panelled thoughout (except for the roof). The number of half-drop windows was increased to five each side upstairs and four downstairs and the front destination boxes were rearranged so that the single-line blind came above instead of below those for the route number and intermediate points. This was doubtless done as the blind needing to be changed most often would have been rather awkward to get at with the more raked front end if it had been left in the bottom position. However, this layout was adopted for the STL11-type bodies (15576-15781) built for the next series (STL1060-1259) part way through the batch. Ostensibly the body 15781 fitted to STL857 was the last of these but in fact it was built first and had the roof ribs in line with the pillars, one per panel, like the STL5 bodies.

STL857 entered service in November 1935. It was shortly afterwards renumbered STF1 but it reverted to its original number at first overhaul in 1937 when a standard body was fitted. The special body was rebuilt to a half cab for use with a normal bonnet and exposed radiator and next appeared on STL1167, a Camberwell Green bus, later in 1937. It remained on STL1167 for the rest of its life and was coded STL11/1. Some years after the war the front end was rebuilt to effectively the standard shape, removing one more touch of variety from the London street scene.

STL1060-1259, which were ordered on sanction DA54 with 206 bodies (15576-15781), were turned into traffic between November 1935 and March 1936. The chassis again incorporated certain modifications (denoted by the code 2/9STL) but most of the increase in licensing weight (now 6T12C) was attributable to the fact that the STL11-type bodies built for this sanction were fully double-panelled and incorporated the new tubular aluminium seats. With these improvements London at last got buses whose interior trim did justice to the elegant outline introduced a year earlier and which ranked with contemporary standards in Birmingham and Manchester. After the first 50 bodies had been built the front destination boxes were rearranged as in the special body for STL857 with the single-line blind above instead of below the route number and intermediate points, incidentally without any distinction by code, and the sidelights were moved from the black band back to the cab front and bulkhead. The roof, which was still single-panelled with joints midway between the pillars, now had two ribs per panel instead of one. This meant that there was no rib in line with pillars — a thing which some people found strange — but the increased stiffness together with the double panelling contributed to an improvement in quietness, even though the engine was still of the Comet Mk 1 type. The STL11 bodies could also be distinguished by having three opening windows on each side of the lower

saloon whereas the STL5-type bodies only had two. In the next batch of buses, STL1264-1463, built against sanction H75 with 206 bodies 16280-16485, the Comet Mk III version of the 7.7-litre engine was introduced. This was slightly less powerful (with a rating of 108bhp instead of 115bhp at 2,000rpm, though some of this drop was attributable to the nominal bore now being 105mm instead of 106mm), slightly quieter, and gave a slightly better fuel consumption. These buses, which all originally had bodies of the STL11-type, were coded 3/9STL11. They entered service between March and July 1936.

STL1246, one of the previous batch, also entered service in July 1936. It had been sent as a new chassis to Leyland to be fitted with a torque converter transmission of the current type which it was proposed to specify in 10 of the STD-type buses delivered the following year. After bodying STL1246 was allocated to Chelverton Road. I do not know how long it ran with the torque converter transmisson before being converted to standard, but my guess would be that this would have been at first overhaul about the beginning of 1938 and the transmission would then have become a spare for STD91-100.

All the changes to both chassis and body described in connection with STL1264-1463 were incorporated in 50 further buses for Country Area, STL1464-1513, built against sanction H76, which appeared in the second half of 1936. The bodies 16670-16719 were an improved version of the first country series, double-panelled and with tubular aluminum seats, and also had the revised front blind arrangements and sidelights

Right:
STL1132, code 2/9STL11, with body having the later arrangement of destination boxes, working from Putney Bridge in 1936. Note the use of two ribs per roof panel. See also page 10. *J. F. Higham*

Left:
STL1506, of the second country series, working from Romford on Green Line service during the early years of the war. Note the busy effect produced by Weymann's use of three ribs per roof panel and the radius at both inner and outer corners of the top front windows. *D. W. K. Jones*

below the waistrail. They were contracted to Weymann of Addlestone which turned out an extremely solid job incorporating metal-framed construction. They were, unfortunately, rather heavy, weighing more than 7 tons with only 48 seats, and even during the war this seating capacity was not increased to 52 as was done with the Chiswick-bodied first country series. However, the Weymann bodies proved to be the best, in terms of lasting qualities, of all the body variants fitted to the STL-type. They could be easily distinguished by the fact that the upper front windows were radiused at both inner and outer corners and by the provision of three ribs for each roof panel, features not found in any of the Chiswick or Park Royal bodies. Practically all this series were allocated to country garages south of the Thames, from Northfleet to Windsor. Sadly, they were the last front-entrance STLs; one feels that the design could have been developed to carry 52 or even 56 seated passengers with little or no weight penalty.

The 500 buses which followed, STL1514-2013, all of them for Central Area, were covered by a single sanction H89 which included no spare bodies. However, the 500 bodies built (16834-17333) included four different specifications. STL1514-1613 were a further batch of 3/9 STL-type buses the standard body for which was still the STL11-type. They entered service between July and October 1936, a notable exception being STL1603 which was used as a chassis for demonstration at garages, much as ST2 had been in 1930-31. It was in fact the last 9STL variant to be licensed, in May 1938.

STL1614-2013, which followed on immediately from the previous series between October 1936 and July 1937, incorporated a modified design of fluid flywheel and the gearbox now had a plate clutch for top gear. The chassis code was accordingly altered to 4/9 STL except for six buses delivered with the new (and then unannounced) toroidal direct-injection version of the 7.7-litre engine (STL1642, 1654, 1657, 1661, 1668 and 1670) which were originally coded 5/9 STL. Later conversions to direct injection, of which there were a large number, were not distinguished by code.

All these 400 buses had Chiswick-built bodies with the STL11-type interior. The majority had a revised destination blind display with the route number box in the roof dome. However, there were 40 bodies (17294-17333) which had a special roof profile for working through the Blackwall Tunnel which had the later STL11-type blind arrangement; these buses only seated 55 as the staircase curved round to meet the upper deck gangway, displacing the adjacent single seat in the process. The tunnel bodies were coded STL13. The normal bodies were of two types which were outwardly indistinguishable. In the STL12-type body the floor framework was fabricated in steel whereas in the STL14 bodies it was in timber, as it had been in the STL11 design. However, although 100 STL12-type bodies were authorised only half a dozen were built at this stage; London Transport was to return to it later.

STL2014-2188 were a further batch of 4/9 STL chassis for Central Area covered by sanction G276, the bodies for which (17435-17609) were contracted to Park Royal Coachworks. Coded STL15, they were delivered between February and September 1937. These bodies were outwardly of the standard roof-indicator type but incorpor-

Above:
STL2248, Code 4/9STL14/1. The Chiswick-built roof-box bodies of codes STL12, 14 and 14/1 were indistinguishable. *LT U29878*

ated Park Royal's metal-framed construction. By the discerning eye they could be distinguished externally by the fact that the beading between the panels was continued up the window pillars, giving them a fluted effect, and internally by the pillar cappings being round instead of flat.

Sadly, the Park Royal bodies did not prove to have the lasting qualities of the Weymann or even, indeed, the timber-framed Chiswick bodies. In their defence it might be argued that they were only designed for a 10-year life but in the situation resulting from the 1939-45 war buses had to last longer than this. Only about 20 of the Park Royal bodies lasted longer than 1948-49 and it was their demise which sparked off the unfortunate conversion of 160 STLs to take RT-type bodies. Had the bodies for these 175 chassis been built at Chiswick it would still have been possible to complete the programme by the works holiday at the end of July 1938.

In the midst of all this activity in producing standard STLs, London Transport placed a contract (sanction G261) with Leyland in 1936 for the supply of 100 complete double-deck buses. Leyland had previously supplied trolleybuses to London

Transport's tram and trolleybus department but this was its first order for full-size buses. Nominally, these were of the Titan TD4 model, but they incorporated many departures from the manufacturer's standard specification for this model, starting with the chassis frames. These were of a new shape at the front where a different design of spring anchorage was used. This was to be adopted as standard on the later TD5 model, but there is some reason to believe that the London Transport contract may have required special frames to suit a wheelbase of 16ft 3in, which Leyland was later to adopt on the TD6 and TD7 models. This may also have underlain the decision to give the type letters STD to these buses instead of continuing with the TD series used for the TD1 and TD2 model Titans inherited from independents.*

Other non-standard features incorporated were a worm and nut steering box (bought in from AEC) and 36 × 8 tyres front and rear. More remarkable perhaps is that London Transport was prepared to

* The Leyland trolleybuses were also produced to AEC standard mean wheelbases of 16ft 6in and 18ft 7in.

accept standard Leyland transmissions in these 100 buses. STD1-90 had friction clutches and crash gearboxes; the latter were, however, quite refined examples of their kind, with helical constant mesh third gear. STD91-100 were originally fitted with Leyland torque converter transmission which we have already met in connection with STL221. All 100 buses were fitted with Leyland's 8.6-litre overhead camshaft oil engines rated at 98bhp at 1,900rpm and standard Leyland axles, the rear axle being of the fully floating type with 7½in centres worm drive of the usual Leyland ratio of 5.4:1.

The STD body also incorporated a number of departures from the standard Leyland metal framed body of the period. This was a five-bay design introduced in 1936. Its outline derived from the standard London Transport trolleybus bodies which were curved front and rear in similar manner to the standard STL bodies which have been described. To assist Leyland in preparing its tender STL1217 was sent there when new in 1936 for several weeks to help the company to understand London Transport's requirements. These included the tubular aluminium seats introduced with the STL11-type (of which STL1217 was an example), rexine-covered lining panels throughout on both decks, the standard London staircase and upper deck seating layout with two single seats (which, along with the doorless cab and bulb horn must have caused some surprise at Leyland) and the standard indicator display in its latest form with the front route number box in the roof dome. This was executed by Leyland with outstanding neatness; their roof, although of single-skin construction, had joints in line with the pillars and one intermediate rib to each panel. It had London Transport's usual longitudinal wooden rails inside, one each side of the gangway. The front followed Leyland's standard contour, but the cab was changed to resemble the STL design very closely, naturally with no door (but a full height doorway), and a valance from the top of the screen pillar to the nearside bulkhead similar to that fitted to the standard STL body was included. The top of the STL-type windscreen was lower than Leyland's standard screen with which a shallower valance was used. The lower edge of the front bulkhead windows was straight, at a height dictated by the bonnet line, the curved lower edge of the STL design not being attempted. All 100 bodies (17335-17434) were the same and coded STD1 although one seat was removed from STD91-100 while they carried their torque converters (presumably at the insistence of the Public Carriage Office). The chassis code of STD1-90 was 1STD and the torque converter-equipped STD91-100, 2STD.

London Transport's willingness in 1937 to accept a clutch and gearbox in these buses is surprising. It probably reflected the fact that the drivers at Hendon, which had previously only had NSs and some early petrol STLs, had never known anything else. This was a totally different situation from that obtaining in Birmingham, for instance, where the torque converter transmission available in the Leyland Titan was seen as an asset for the conversion of tram routes to bus operation. Even so, it always appeared to me that London Transport was very unadventurous in not going for the Gearless transmission on these buses when it was an available and well-established option. STD91, the first of the 10 torque converter-

equipped buses was, in fact, the first bus of the order to be delivered, being received at Chiswick in March 1937 although it was not sent to Hendon until July after all its crash-box sisters were in service. I can remember being told at Chiswick that some development work was done on the transmission including the provision of a positive neutral which it had previously lacked (although this may have been on STL1246). However, the torque converter transmissions were removed from all of STD91-100 during 1939, either at their first overhaul in the summer or in the case of STD97 and 99 in December and November respectively, when crash gearboxes were substituted. The memory I have of riding up Fleet Street on one of these 10 buses when working on route 13 in 1937 or 1938 is one which I realise few readers of this book will share.

Having a crash gearbox did not prevent most of the 100 STD-type buses surviving until 1953-54. The Leyland bodies proved to have excellent lasting qualities. These buses spent practically all their lives at Hendon, where they were well liked, and only during the war were any moved elsewhere when at various times some ran from Cricklewood, Gillingham Street and Edgware. After the re-equipment of Hendon in 1952 many were moved to Enfield to replace wartime Guys.

Construction of standard STLs with Chiswick bodies continued meanwhile with a further 327 buses, STL2189-2515, ordered against sanction G280 which also covered the first 150 coaches of the 10T10 type. The original sanction appears to have covered only 327 bodies, 17634-17960, of which the first 233 were of code STL14/1 and the last 94 were the balance of code STL12. However, 12 spare bodies were also built, apparently on a later authorisation; these were of the STL14/1-type and were built at the time of the changeover between the two

designs in November and December 1937, although they were numbered 18076-18087 after 115 numbers which had been reserved at that stage, presumably for the bodies for the next batch of STLs which eventually received numbers in the new series.

STL2189-2515 were all coded 4/9STL; however STL2513, 2514, and 2515 did not originally have engines of the standard 7.7-litre Comet Mk III-type but instead had prototype engines of a new 8.8-litre design, unit number A182. Although this had the same bore and stroke as the established 8.8-litre engine (a direct-injection version of which was about to appear in the 10T10-type coaches) the A182 engine was a completely new design which despite an increase of 10mm in the cylinder centre distance achieved compactness by the use of a geared timing case and V-belt drive for the fan and water pump. It is known that the A182 engines fitted in STL2513, 2514 and 2515 (which were probably the first three produced) were flexibly mounted but otherwise little is known about this installation. Some dispensation on overall length may have been needed, as the bodies were standard examples of the STL12-type, but probably only 1½in or 2in. The purpose of trying them in these buses was to gain service experience with the engine which — at this stage — it was intended to use in the RT-type. STL2513, 2514 and 2515 entered service at Hanwell in April and May 1938 after the bulk of STL2189-2512 which appeared between June 1937 and March 1938. Three stragglers, STL1603, 2348 and 2467 which were not placed in traffic until May and June were the last new AEC buses with indirect-injection engines to enter service.

The A182 engines in STL2514 and 2515 were replaced with standard 7.7-litre units in January 1942 and April 1943 respectively.

STL2513 was given a 9.6-litre engine (presumably a version of the A185 prewar RT engine) in December 1943 and did not receive a 7.7-litre engine until March 1944. From then on all three buses were standard examples of code 4/9STL12.

The A180 engine used in the 10T10-type coaches (and later the LT-type), the A182 engines just mentioned and the later A185 (9.6-litre) engine used in the RT-type all employed the Leyland pot type direct-injection combustion system, discussed at greater length in the examination of the vehicles in question in succeeding chapters. It was experience with this system in the STD-type which achieved this impact on London Transport's thinking, although nine inherited TD-type buses with similar engines had been operated for some years. The pot type combustion system used needed about 5% less fuel for a given amount of work than the Comet Mk III system and allowed starting from cold without heater plugs. However, it required a bigger engine capacity for a given torque; this prevented its easy adoption in the STL-type whereas the toroidal direct-injection system now available from AEC was almost as good as the Comet Mk III system in this respect and gave a still better specific fuel consumption. Consequently the A182 engines fitted in STL2513, 2514 and 2515 were the only ones using the pot type combustion system ever fitted to STL-type buses apart from the 12 Godstone vehicles as converted from 1940 onwards.

The 12 spare bodies 18076-18087 built at the end of 1937 represented the entire provision for the 1,002 buses STL1514-2515. This drop in the provision of spares reflects the extension of the overhaul period to two

years and it must be remembered that the 23 spares built for STL609-958 could also be drawn upon, any of these bodies being applicable to any of the 9STL derivatives. No spares were built for STL2516-2647 although three were provided for the 266 10T10-type coaches (a new departure) and a further 12 STL bodies were built in 1941 to ease shortages resulting from enemy action.

After an interval of several months a further batch of 132 STLs was ordered to replace the remaining buses of the TD-type (Leyland Titans of models TD1 and TD2). London Transport's return showed 140 double-deck examples of this type as still being in stock at 30 June 1938, including 20 in Country Area, although not all those in Central Area stock were still required for service. Accordingly the building of 115 buses (STL2516-2630, with bodies 88-202) was authorised on sanction G305 which also included the 10T10/1-type coaches T603-718, TF2-88 and CR-49. However, to allow for increasing traffic in Country Area and consequent conversion of routes from single- to double-deck operation 17 further buses (STL2631-2647, with bodies 207-223) were included in the next sanction raised, G325, which also covered RT2-151. Of the resulting total of 132 buses STL2516-2647, Country Area's share was 39.

STL2516-2647, coded 15STL16, incorporated a number of improvements on previous STLs and represented the ultimate development of the AEC Regent in its original concept. The engines were of the 7.7-litre toroidal direct-injection type flexibly-mounted in the chassis by means of a two-point 'floating power' suspension. This meant the disappearance of the familiar protruding starter dog and the opportunity was taken to provide a handsome new radiator, deeper than before, which the numberplate straddled instead of hanging down below it. Automatic brake adjusters and automatic chassis lubrication were other novel chassis features. The dynamo was driven by V-belts at the front of the gearbox instead of the previous chain drive. The bodies incorporated detail changes, a tell-tale one being the mounting of the stop and tail lights in a detachable panel above the rear number plate.

If not by London Transport's sixth birthday on 1 July 1939, by the beginning of September — the end of an era for Europe — there were, with six exceptions, only four types of double-deck bus in the fleet: the LT-type, with 1,222 examples; the ST-type, with 1,137; the STL-type, with 2,625 and the STD-type, with 100. This was a remarkable triumph for Rackham, who had designed all the AEC chassis as well as the original Titan from which the STD-type was descended.

The standard STLs remained in service until 1953-54. Those which were converted to SRT-type in 1948-49 — mainly former 15STL16-type buses of the STL2516-2647 series — lasted little, if any, longer than those which escaped this treatment. The displaced STL16 bodies were mostly mounted on chassis which had previously carried Park Royal bodies and these were coded 19STL16/2. As well as this major reconstruction programme there was an extensive dynamo drive conversion pro-gramme, substituting a V-belt drive for the original chain drive in the gearbox, which was applied to the whole series from STL609 to 2515 from 1945 onwards. Many of the A171 engines, whether Comet Mk I or Mk III were also converted to A173 (toroidal direct-injection) in postwar years. During the war seven buses received wartime bodies — which but for the seats were virtually of the standard roof-box pattern (code STL17) — from a batch of 12 produced in 1941 to ease the shortage caused by blitz casualties; 20 received Chiswick-built wartime lowbridge bodies (code STL19) and one, STL932, of the more utilitarian normal-height STL17/1-type produced to make up the balance of 34 bodies needed to match the unfrozen Regent chassis with crash gearboxes which London Transport received in 1941-42. All these wartime bodies had wooden-framed seats of the type used in the Bluebirds and early STLs. STL2150 received a body of the pre-standard (STL18) type and many migrations of bodies of standard type took place between the batches of standard chassis.

Two Central Area buses were chosen for successive pay-as-you-board experiments after the war for which purposes their staircases and entrances (and separate exits), were moved to the front. Finally, STL2477 was chosen to receive the last body built at Chiswick. Of prefabricated construction and known as Mr Sainsbury's body after its designer, it was true to the Chiswick tradition in having no cab door.

Below:
STL2580, code 15STL16, at Greenford when new in 1939. The 132 buses of this series, which incorporated various refinements and represented the ultimate development of the STL-type, were split between Central and Country Areas, 93 going to Hanwell and Alperton and 39 to Northfleet and Dartford.
LT U29484

London Transport's requirements for single-deck vehicles in the 1930s fell into four distinct categories. These were respectively, 20-seater service buses designed for one-man operation; full size service buses seating 30 or more; coaches for the Green Line services, and coaches for other purposes such as private hire, sightseeing tours and the Inter-Station services introduced in 1936.

In the mid-1930s London Transport had a total requirement for some 170 20-seaters. 65 of these were operated in Central Area, mostly in the Romford-Hornchurch district where Central Area came closest to the London Transport boundary. The 42 Dennis Darts of the DA-type built between 1930 and 1932 catered for the LGOC's share of this business.

The chassis which London Transport chose as a basis for its standard 20-seater was the Leyland Cub, which was built in Leyland's factory at Kingston-upon-Thames. As originally introduced in 1932 it had a 15ft 6in wheelbase and a six-cylinder side-valve petrol engine of 3⅜in bore and 5in stroke giving a swept volume of 4.4 litres. One of these early Cubs came to London Transport's Country Area from the St Albans & District undertaking. This bus received the number C76 and the code

1/1C1/1 when the country buses were numbered in 1935. In LPTB days it was operated from Slough and Windsor before it was sold in 1939.

In 1934 some redesign of the Cub chassis took place and a 14ft wheelbase model, KP2, was introduced. The 15ft 6in model chosen by London Transport became KP3. At this stage the only engine was still the same side-valve petrol unit. The first Cub bought by London Transport, C1, was of this specification. It was ordered on a Central Area sanction, D20, and completed in June 1934 with a Chiswick-built body (14756) of composite construction with a sliding passenger door which could be worked by the driver from his seat. The seats were of the contemporary plywood-framed type. Coded 1C1, C1 was placed in service at Hornchurch.

In August 1934 the purchase of 74 Cubs for Country Area was sanctioned (sanction E24). By this time a diesel engine had become available and this was specified for C2-75. This engine had the same bore and stroke, 3⅜in and 5in, as the side-valve petrol engine and therefore the same swept volume of 4.4 litres. It employed the pot type direct-injection combustion system as used in the Leyland 8.1 and 8.6-litre oil engines and thus equipped gave a rated

Below:
C76, code 1/1C1/1, ex-St Albans & District, working from Windsor in 1938. This bus originally had a short radiator and the sidelamps mounted on top of the front wings. *J. F. Higham*

output of 55bhp at 2,200rpm. Despite its modest power this engine had the advantage that it would start from cold without heater plugs. The bodies of these buses (14916-14989) were built by Short Bros of Rochester — the first and last contract placed with this company by London Transport. The design of these bodies was generally similar to that of C1 but they were of metal-framed construction and incorporated an offside emergency door. Coded 2C2, these buses entered service during the spring of 1935. Many which were no longer required at the end of the war were then sold to the Allied Control Commission for Europe but the remainder lasted until the 1950s.

While at Hornchurch C1 was fitted in June 1935 with a Perkins Leopard four-cylinder oil engine. In November 1935 it was transferred to Country Area in exchange for C51, which was then fitted with a newly introduced version of the Leyland light six oil engine of 3½in bore and 5in stroke. This engine had an indirect injection combustion system and gave a rated power of 65bhp — an increase dictated by Leyland's desire to use it in the Cheetah model announced at the 1935 Commercial Motor Show. With this engine C51 was recoded 1/2C2.

The increase in bore size was the largest which could be accommodated within the constraints of the original Leyland Light Six engine design and increased the swept volume from 4.4 to 4.7 litres. At the same time the alternative petrol engine was also redesigned. In its new form it was an overhead-valve unit of 3½in bore × 5in stroke. The chassis designations now became KPZ3 and KPZ03. A forward control, or side type, version was also introduced (SKPZ). The indirect injection engine was

chosen for 22 further Cubs for Central Area delivered in 1936. The bodies for these were contracted to Weymann as Shorts had by this time withdrawn from bus body manufacture. They were coded 1/2C2/1. The original sanction, H62, was for 20 buses C77-96 with body numbers 16131-16150. However, two additional buses, C97 and 98, were covered by sanction H79 which also included Q186 and 187, two vehicles of coach specification for Country Area. C97 and 98 had bodies numbered 16254-5.

The use of 20-seaters in Central Area came to an end during the 1939-45 war and the majority of these buses which were delicensed when the war ended were then sold to the Allied Control Commission. The remainder spent the rest of their lives in Country Area, lasting until 1953. C76 was sold in January 1939 after exchanging its petrol engine for the Perkins oil engine from C1. C1, once again petrol-engined, was sold in 1946.

For the Inter-Station services introduced in 1936 London Transport ordered eight forward control Cubs on sanction H90. These were completed with special Park Royal coach bodies, 16722-9, having a large luggage locker under a raised rear portion, a layout to which Park Royal returned for airport coaches after the war. Numbered C106-113, these eight coaches had 3½in bore overhead valve petrol engines and were coded 3C3. They were painted in a striking livery of pale blue and primrose with a black roof. When the Inter-Station services were suspended during the early part of the war these coaches were used by ENSA to whom the large luggage locker was useful for carrying scenery and properties. Three ST-type buses, ST164, 454 and 470 were painted in the blue and primrose

livery towards the end of the war to resume the service, but the Cubs returned to Old Kent Road soon after the war ended. At the time of their withdrawal in 1953 they were the last petrol-engined buses operated by London Transport. The numbers C99-105 were never used for buses. There were seven works lorries numbered C99L-105L on Leyland Cub chassis which as far as is known were never intended for bus use.

Coming now to full-size single-deck service buses, the Central Area's requirement was largely satisfied by the 199 LT and 60 T-type buses (the latter figure including three Chiswick chassis and 12 former Tilling-operated vehicles) inherited from the LGOC. At the vesting date these were all less than four years old and as a result, during the period here under review the number of new single-deck buses which had to be bought to replace miscellaneous inherited vehicles in the Central Area was only 53.

The position in Country Area however was very different; not only were single-deckers required for a larger proportion of duties but the inherited vehicles formed a very heterogeneous collection. The largest number of one model were ADC416s of which there were 90, nearly all of ESTC or National origin. These dated from 1926-28 and although on pneumatic tyres belonged to the pre-Rackham era and were clearly candidates for early replacement. It was principally for this purpose that the purchase of 100 single-deckers for Country Area was authorised in the latter part of 1934 on sanction E25.

To the surprise of many people — not least at AEC — the model chosen was the AEC Q-type in its 18ft 6in wheelbase form with A170 Comet Mk I oil engine, fluid transmission and Lockheed brakes. The contract for the bodies (14990-15089) was awarded to the Birmingham Railway Carriage & Wagon Co, a new supplier for London Transport. The bodies were of a distinctive design with sloping roof and in deference to Country Area wishes featured a central entrance with sliding door. The emergency door was amidships on the offside. As first delivered these bodies seated 37 but this was shortly reduced to 35 by the incorporation of a full-width partition behind the driver. The seats were of the lightweight wooden type introduced with the Bluebirds; eight of them were sideways facing, over the engine and front wheel arches. The use of sideways-facing seats over the rear wheelarches was avoided by raising them on footstools.

Delivered in the spring of 1935, these vehicles were numbered Q6-105. The first 75 were finished to the basic specification described, classified as buses (suffix B) and coded 4Q4; however, the last 25 vehicles were given luggage racks, saloon heaters and brackets for side route boards. When Country Area received 27 doorless front entrance buses from the next sanction in 1936 these vehicles were classified as coaches, code 1/4Q41, and suffixed C, together with two similar vehicles, Q186 and 187, delivered in 1936. These formed the balance of another of the strange sanctions for only four buses, H79, which we have already met in conjunction with C97 and 98. This was perhaps the strangest sanction of all, covering two Leyland Cubs for Central Area and the two Q-types for Country Area. The bodies for Q186 and 187, 16256 and 16257, were also built by the Birmingham Railway Carriage & Wagon Co.

In reality the only claim these vehicles had to be suitable for Green Line use was the inclusion of a saloon door and a heater. The seats were barely comfortable enough for a passenger to occupy for an hour or more, as Green Line passengers often had to, and the noise level from the Comet Mk I engine was rather high. The need for 27 coaches arose from the rebodying as buses of 30 Reliances previously classified as coaches, discussed at more length in Chapter 11. The fact that the 1/4Q4/1s were minimally suitable for use as coaches was conceded by confining them as far as possible to the shorter routes such as Golders Green-Watford and Grays-Aldgate, and they were all reclassified as buses when the TF-type coaches entered service in 1939.

The bodies built for Q6-105, 186, 187 and the 43 bodies built by Weymann for rebodying Reliance and Regal chassis are interesting architecturally. They embodied a transitional style, not seen in any double-deck design. The STL and STD-type bodies continued to use square-cornered windows retained by wooden sill strips, a style which came in with the first Bluebird design body built for LT741. However, in these single-deck bodies the windows were fixed in pans with rounded corners but the pillar spacing was still relatively narrow, allowing the same type of half-drop windows, worked with a central grip, to be used. Another feature appearing for the first time in single-deck bodies in these designs was an angle between the upper and lower portions

of the windscreen, following the line of curved pillars; although in less marked degree, this was already in use in the standard STL design.

In subsequent single-deck bodies both for buses and coaches and later in the RT-type a wider pillar spacing was adopted. This necessitated a winding mechanism for the half-drop windows which controlled the position of the window at both sides and prevented the risk of jamming. These windows were also fitted in pans with rounded corners. The first vehicles in which these features were seen were the next order for 80 Q-type buses, Q106-185, ordered on sanction H61 with body Nos 16151-16230, which were delivered in the spring of 1936. In these vehicles the wheelbase was reduced to 16ft 6in, the front overhang being increased (as in the double-deck model) to accommodate the entrance, which had no door. The floor and waistline were both higher than in the 4Q4-type, so that out of 37 seats only seven were longitudinal, two over the nearside front wheel and five over the engine and offside front wheel. The seats were of the tubular aluminium type, by now standard in STL bodies. The bodies were built by Park Royal and were of metal-framed construction. In this design a central rear emergency door was adopted. Unusually, this batch was split between Central and Country Areas, Central Area receiving 53 and Country Area 27, the latter making good the appropriation of 1/4Q4/1-type vehicles for coaches.

Q106-185 were coded 5Q5. Having no entrance door there was no question of these vehicles being used as coaches but with their high seating capacity they made excellent service buses. Their layout allowed driver control of boarding and alighting and I have never heard it

Left:
C83, code 1/2C2/1, one of the Weymann-bodied buses built for Central Area in 1936. *J. F. Higham*

113

suggested that the doorless entrance created a safety problem. Their layout would have permitted one-man operation but I do not believe this capability was ever exploited during their lifetime. The 53 Central Area examples were the only Q-type single-deckers to spend their whole lives in the Central Area. A touch of distinction was given to these buses when they were new by painting the roof and rear dome black.

With their long front and short rear overhangs they were rather strange to drive and amongst Cricklewood drivers, at least, they were known as crabs. This name graphically conveys the impression received from the driving seat during a tight turn. By the time they had been in service for a while it became apparent that the Q-type in its diesel-engined single-deck form was a very satisfactory design of bus for its time and economical to maintain. London Transport never had occasion to regret its decision to adopt it as its standard single-deck bus in the mid-1930s. These buses survived until the arrival of the RF-type in 1952-53.

The LPTB Report for 1936 also showed 87 Gilfords in service as coaches which were next in line for replacement. This objective was achieved by the purchase of 50 Regal and 50 Q-type coaches on sanction H87 and downgrading 12 petrol-engined Regals, T346-357, which had been rebodied the previous year, to country buses. The Regals came first, in the summer of 1936. Numbered T403-452, they corresponded closely in chassis specification with the contemporary STL-type double-deckers, having 7.7-litre Comet Mk III engines, fluid flywheels, D132 preselective gearboxes, fully floating rear axles with a ratio of 5.2;1 and servo-assisted Lockheed brakes. The wheelbase was 17ft 6in and the overall length 27ft 6in. The bodies, numbered 16620-16669, were of a new London Transport design although built by Weymann using their metal-framed construction. Thirty seats were provided, all facing forward, the last four rows being raised on footstools, although with two internal steps the floor was at a height which cleared the flywheel housings. The seats were of the new tubular aluminium type as used in contemporary STL bodies. Double-skinned throughout, the bodies were of a five-bay design with winding windows of which the last two on each side were at a higher level than the first three. The passenger door at the front slid into an internal compartment and there was a central rear emergency door. An unusual feature which was not to be repeated in any later design was that not only the nearside wing but the whole bonnet was carried on the body. This was tied to the cab by a valance below the radiator, which was surrounded by an all-round gaiter. In front of the valance was a bumper; as an appendage to the 9T9 this was probably more ornamental than useful, but it was to have a value to London Transport which could not be foreseen at the time, which was that it increased the effective bonnet length which had to be allowed for in the design of the body. It was thus one of the things which made it possible two years later to incorporate the 8.8-litre engine in the 10T10 design with a body having the same pillar spacing and windows.

The 9T9s were rather overshadowed by the 10T10s after the arrival of the latter in 1938 and although they were good and trouble-free coaches they were seldom seen in Green Line service after demobilisation from ambulance duty at the end of the war. The totals shown in the London Transport Report for 30 June 1939, if this is to be believed, indicate that 29 of these vehicles had already been reclassified as country buses. They were withdrawn in 1952.

The Q-type was less satisfactory as a basis for a coach than a bus because even with a high floor the chassis layout dictated some number of longitudinal seats over the engine. Nevertheless the 50 purpose-built coaches for the Green Line services, Q189-238, which were delivered during the winter of 1936-37 were a great improvement on the 1/4Q4/1-type. Coded 6Q6, these were based on the 18ft 6in wheelbase chassis, as it was desired to have the entrance behind the front wheel where a sliding door could be accommodated. A higher floor level was adopted than in either the 4Q4 or 5Q5 designs so that all the seats could be forward facing except for four over the engine which were provided with individual armrests. With a rear emergency door 32 seats were accommodated and these were of the tubular aluminium type now standardised. The engines in Q189-238 were of the Comet Mk III type which besides giving a better fuel consumption were slightly quieter. The bodies (16730-16779), which were metal-framed, were built by Park Royal. All told, Q189-238 made fairly civilised coaches, even though the seats over the engine were nearly always the last to be occupied, and they maintained the service between Hertford and Guildford (their home garages) for many years both before and after the war until displaced by the RF-type. During the war they served as ambulances. Q217 was a wartime casualty, but the other 49 vehicles survived until the 1950s.

The story of the Q-type ends with a kind of final fling in the shape of Q188. Covered by sanction H63, Q188 was in every way an exception. It was built on a three-axle chassis, the only one ever built (chassis No 0763001) to which the driveline layout lent itself quite well, single wheels naturally being used at the rear. It was also double-decked, being one of a series of experimental double-deck coaches built for trial on the Green Line services at intervals over the years by London Transport and the LGOC before it, beginning with LT1137 in 1931. It was, in fact, an exact successor to LT1137, its Park Royal body seating 51. The styling of the body (16130) bore some resemblance to the full-fronted body built for STL857 and described in Chapter 9. However, the lower deck windows were with rounded corners, in the manner of contemporary single-deck coach bodies, and those on the upper deck were grouped in pairs. It had a non-standard indicator

Above:
**Q129, code 5Q5, with Park Royal
doorless front entrance body.
One of the Central Area examples
of this type, July 1936.**
LT U20008

display consisting of three blind boxes one above the other, although from photographs it appears that the one in the middle may have accepted the standard single-deck blind. The ones above and below were both shallow and would only accept a single-line blind or an illuminated sign. A rear-hinged cab door was provided for the driver's entry, a foot hole being provided in front of the front wheel. The tyres were of the size used on the Q-type single-deckers, 10.50-20 and not of the larger size, 11.25-20, used on the four-wheeled double-deckers. Whether this was a help or a hindrance to the staff at Hertford when Q188 entered service with Q2, 3, 4 and 5 can, at this distance, only be a matter for conjecture. The chassis was received at Chiswick on 19 May 1936; Q188 was received back from Park Royal with the body mounted on 1 February 1937 and spent from 23 March until 9 June that year at AEC. Coded 7Q7, it was not licensed until 1 June 1938. Shortly afterwards it was sent to Hertford where it was used on the 310 service to Waltham Cross along with Q2-5. As far as I know Q188 was never used on the Green Line services during its time at Hertford. It had an oil engine of the Comet Mk III type and, according to the rolling

stock card, compressed air brakes. Both rear axles were driven with the usual AEC three-differential drive. Q188 was moved to Grays in July 1939 in company with Q2-5 and with them it was delicensed shortly after the outbreak of war. Sold by London Transport in 1946, it was bought by Gareloch Motor Services of Garelochhead who used it for some years on their service between there and Helensburgh. During this time it must have earned more revenue than it ever did with London Transport.

Following the replacement of the Gilfords the inherited coach fleet remaining in 1937 consisted of six ex-Battens Reliances; 39 Tigers and 19 ex-Premier Titans; a few oddments including five Dennis Lancets and the Daimler DST6 and 284 Regals. The Regals included 23 all-weather coaches with swing doors which were unsuitable for use on the Green Line services, and as they dated from 1930 and 1931 they were getting a bit elderly for private hire and sightseeing tours. In 1937, if the possibility was considered at all, the time was judged to be past when it would have been worth fitting new bodies to these chassis. However, it was becoming apparent that the entire fleet of inherited coaches would have to be replaced over the next two years. Replacements would also be needed for the 27 vehicles of the 1/4Q4/1-type which were in Green Line service to allow these to be downgraded to country buses. The most urgent need was to renew the private hire and sightseeing tours fleet; this was a much less captive market than the Green Line services and it was clearly unsatisfactory for vehicles to be allocated to it for no other reason than that they were unsuitable for Green Line service.

Thus it was that 24 new private hire coaches were bought in 1937. Covered by sanction G283 the vehicles in question, LTC1-24, were intended to replace T150-154, the LGOC private hire coaches of 1930; T393-398, the East Surrey private hire coaches of 1930; T399-402 and 319-324, the East Surrey coaches of 1931, and T360 and 363, ex-Lewis vehicles of 1930, all of which had sun-saloon bodies with swing doors. Another candidate for replacement was DST6, a Daimler CH6 of 1931 vintage which had a handsome Duple sliding-roof body with a front sliding door but still had its original sleeve-valve engine. Since March 1935 it had been the only Daimler in the London Transport fleet.

For the new private hire coaches the Model 663 Renown chassis was chosen. With a mean wheelbase of 16ft 6in this only allowed an overall length of 27ft because the rear overhang was limited by Construction & Use Regulations to half the mean wheelbase. As a result, the LTC-type coaches were actually slightly shorter than the 9T9-type Regals. The choice of the three-axle chassis seems to have been made in the belief that a better ride would thereby be obtained which, the argument ran, would increase the market appeal of these coaches: a somewhat doubtful proposition. The reason for which practically all other British three-axle passenger chassis were bought in the late 1930s, of qualifying for the 30ft length limit and gaining an extra row of seats, was disregarded. This is hard to understand; one would have thought that there would often have been occasions on which it would have been useful to have 24 coaches available with 34 or 38 seats, on Derby day for example.

The chassis number of LTC1 followed on immediately from LT1426 built five years earlier. Because new frames had to be ordered specially for the LTC-type, the opportunity was taken to change the shape to straight instead of dropped at the rear end.

LTC1-24 were completed with handsome bodies (17610-17633) of very similar design to the 9T9-type and like them, built by Weymann and provided with an internal sliding door. The specification included a rigid sliding roof, radio and 30 coach-type seats. A single destination box, of the standard single-deck type, was provided at the front only.

The unladen weight was prodigious — 8ton 5cwt. One cannot help thinking that it would have been possible to have built a 30ft long vehicle with one or even two extra rows of seats within this figure. The power train consisted of 110mm bore A145 petrol engines and fluid transmission, with which the axle ratio originally used was 6.75:1. The rear axles themselves were of the fully floating type, the bogie being essentially as redesigned in 1935 for use in trolleybuses with 8in centres worm drive differentials. A single 45gal fuel tank was fitted on the offside.

The use of a petrol engine was also decided upon in the belief that it would enhance passenger appeal. The arrangement made was an interesting throwback to that adopted for the STLs delivered in

Left:
T414, code 9T9, one of 50 coaches for which the bodies were built by Weymann in 1936. In their mechanical specification they were an exact counterpart of the contemporary STL-type, with Comet Mk III combustion system, a feature which they shared with the 6Q6-type coaches ordered against the same sanction. A unique detail was that the bonnet was carried on the body. Seen here in Weybridge working as a country bus in postwar days.
Author

1933-34; the petrol engines fitted were reconditioned units removed from LT-type vehicles and 24 A165 8.8-litre Comet Mk 1 engines were supplied loose by AEC for fitting to LT-type vehicles. The return for 30 June 1937 given in London Transport's 1937 report shows that 12 of them had already been fitted, some months before the coaches appeared in November.

The LTC-type coaches after serving as ambulances during the war were afterwards used intermittently on the Green Line services. By this time they had been fitted with standard tubular aluminium seats. In 1950 they were converted to diesel using 8.8-litre direct injection engines from scrapped LT-type buses for use with which the axle ratio was changed to 5.8:1. Having seen quite extensive service during the Festival of Britain in 1951 they were sold for scrap in 1953-54.

By the autumn of 1937 the need was also approaching for the replacement of all the remaining inherited coaches which were still in use on the Green Line services. These included 250 of the original Regals with which the services were begun in 1930-31; the two Bucks Expresses, T391/2; nine other

Regals (T358, 359, 361/2, 364-8) inherited from Aston, Amersham and Lewis, and six Reliances inherited from Battens. There were also the 19 ex-Premier Titans, five Dennis Lancets and 39 Tigers as well as the 27 1/4Q4/1s which were substandard for coach use in terms of comfort and noise level.

It was decided to divide the replacement business between AEC and Leyland. 266 Regal chassis were ordered from AEC for delivery in 1938, leaving 87 TF-type chassis to be ordered from Leyland for delivery during 1939. The TF-type is dealt with in detail in the next chapter. There was no need to buy any new single-deck buses as there would be more than enough available by downgrading the 27 1/4Q4/1s and various ex-Green Line front entrance Regals.

The 266 Regals of 1938 were to become famous as the 10T10-type. The 10T10-type was a development of 9T9; the bodies were very similar in appearance but were built at Chiswick and incorporated timber framing. They had a more sophisticated ventilation system and the saloon door slid in a recess on the outside instead of an internal

Below:
Q237, code 6Q6. These Park Royal-bodied coaches spent practically their whole working lives on the Hertford-Guildford Green Line route. When they were replaced on this service by new RF-type coaches in 1952 some of them worked for a time from Muswell Hill, allowing 21-year-old LT-type single-deckers to be withdrawn. *Author*

Above:
Q188, code 7Q7, working from Hertford on Route 310 during its short period in revenue-earning service in 1938-39. *J. F. Higham*

compartment. However, the most important differences were in the chassis. London Transport wanted to incorporate the Leyland pot type combustion system in its new coaches, having been impressed by the smooth running of the Leyland engines in the STD-type double-deckers. However, this meant a bigger engine if the rated power was not to be less than 100bhp, the minimum considered acceptable. AEC had the 8.8-litre engine which could be, and was, redesigned to incorporate the pot type combustion system. This involved new cylinder heads and also a new cylinder block, which had to be taller to allow room for the deep combustion chamber in the piston above the gudgeon pin. As the cylinder block was separate from the crankcase the latter was unaltered. However, the 8.8-litre engine was longer than the 7.7-litre and in all previous installations the bonnet length had had to be increased by some 4½in. This could not be done with a body of the dimensions of the 9T9 without exceeding the permitted overall length.

The problem was solved by design ingenuity at AEC. Because the chassis were

only to have fluid transmission there was no need to make provision for an engine-mounted dynamo. The water pump could therefore be moved from the front to the back of the timing case and the fan, which was the only other component in front of the timing case, could be deleted because of the lower rejection of heat to the cooling water of the direct injection engine. A special radiator was accordingly designed which fitted right up against the timing case. The bottom tank had to be moved downwards to a position in front of the sump with the result that the radiator was noticeably deeper. The number plate was accordingly moved from a position underneath the bottom tank to one straddling the grille. By these means the overall length from the bulkhead to the front of the radiator was reduced to a figure within an inch of the standard length with the petrol or 7.7-litre engine. Deletion of the bumper and valance below the radiator fitted to the 9T9 made it possible to accommodate a body of the same length.

Construction of 150 coaches T453-602 was authorised by sanction G290 to follow

Right:
LTC17, working from Epping in Green Line service in 1947.
Author

Below right:
T711, code 10T10/1, one of the later examples of these much-liked coaches with 34-seat body. Seen at Golders Green in 1947, deputising for the usual TF on Route 713. *Author*

the order for 327 STL-type buses with Chiswick bodies (STL2189-2525) in 1938. Construction of 116 coaches T603-718 with three spare bodies was authorised by sanction G305 which also included TF2-88 and STL2516-2630. Although these vehicles were always known as the 10T10-type there were, in fact, ultimately five variations. T453-577 and 603-718 had 5.2:1 axles and these were chassis code 10T, but T578-602 were (originally at least) provided with 6.25;1 axles, considered necessary to enable them to take off on Titsey and Westerham hills with a full load, and these were distinguished by the code 1/10T. The 150 bodies built for the first sanction, 18096-18245, had 30 seats, the layout being identical with T403-452, and these were body code T10. In the 119 bodies built against sanction G305 (18247-18365) the seat spacing was reduced to allow another row to be squeezed in so that they seated 34 and these were body code T10/1. With the reduced spacing the width of the step well had to be reduced and the screen in front of the first seat altered to match. These changes were not apparent from the outside when the door was closed as the door itself was not altered. However, there was a coincidental detail change to the guttering at the side of the rear dome which enabled the T10/1 body to be distinguished by the sharp-eyed.

Even when new the change from T10 to T10/1 bodies did not occur cleanly between T602 and 603. Moreover, with spares being available T10/1 bodies were later to be found on chassis which had not carried them originally and vice versa. The perceptive reader will have noticed that the 150 30-seat bodies matched the number of 27-seat rear-entrance Green Line Regals T51-149, 155 and 157-206, and the 116 34-seaters the later vehicles which seated 30 or more.

The 10T10-type was one of those happy designs which were a success from all points of view and these vehicles were liked by everyone who came into contact with them. They lasted on the Green Line services until the advent of the RF-type in 1951, when some of them were painted red and used as buses in the Central Area. The last were withdrawn in 1954.

The 1938 London Transport return shows eight petrol-engined Regal coaches as being in service in the Central Area. Six of these were the Strachan-bodied ex-Amersham coaches T359, 361/2 and 364-6, and a seventh was T367, an ex-Lewis coach of 1932, which had a Harrington coach body with sliding roof and also a sliding door. It seems probable that T368 was intended to be the eighth but it was in fact sold in May 1938. These coaches, together with four or five Tigers, were retained during the 1938 season for private hire and sightseeing tours, a duty taken over by the special-bodied TF 'Greenhouses' the following year.

11: Conversions and Rebodyings, 1931-39

There was hardly a time during the 1930s when the LGOC or the LPTB was not engaged in a conversion programme on one type of vehicle or another. This was a consequence of three things, the first of which was what has been called the development explosion which began with the appointment of Rackham at AEC. This resulted in — to quote the most obvious example — new engines which gave enormously improved operating economy becoming available for recent models of bus at a stage when they had plenty of life expectancy left. Secondly, the LGOC had a very strong engineering function, which the LPTB inherited, which was capable of assessing the economics of applying a conversion programme to a whole fleet of buses. The third factor was the LGOC's and later, LPTB's factory overhaul method, involving removal of the body from the chassis every one or two years, which made it all so much easier to carry a conversion programme into effect.

A distinction has to be drawn between a conversion programme which was designed to secure a service benefit, such as enhanced economy or eliminating an unsatisfactory feature, and migrations of equipment which occurred merely or primarily for the convenience of the works. We have seen examples of such migrations involving brake equipment and transmissions. For some reason they seemed to occur only between petrol-engined chassis in the 1930s, even when diesel-engined types were passing through the works in considerable numbers.

Possibly the first conversion programme to be applied to the buses described in this book was the substitution of an AEC worm and nut steering box for the Marles cam and roller unit originally fitted to the ST, T and LT-types delivered before some date towards the end of 1930. The number of vehicles originally fitted with the Marles unit is not easy to assess with accuracy more than 50 years later but it certainly included

Below:
Scene at The Cricketers, Mitcham, in September 1934. All the buses in this picture have received conversions at Chiswick in varying degree. LT247 is still petrol-engined but has the enlarged destination box fitted to LGOC ST and the earlier LT-type bodies in 1932. LT1316 has been converted to diesel and has acquired the characteristic snout of buses fitted with the 8.8-litre engine. NS629 has received in turn a covered top deck, pneumatic tyres and windscreen. *LT U15563*

ST1-301 and 502-516, T1-155, LT1-50 and possibly LT51-150. The substitution of the worm and nut unit, though straightforward, must have involved effectively disposing of the Marles unit at scrap value and the LGOC seems to have been much more ready to do this than some other purchasers of contemporary AEC chassis.

As for converting the D119 gearbox with sliding mesh third gear to the D124-type with constant mesh, this was a matter of fitting a kit within the existing casing; the chassis involved were probably pretty much the same ones.

The conversion of the earlier Regals and Regents from single to triple servo seems to have been a bigger job and to have taken place over a much longer period. The General ST-type buses were undoubtedly built with three servos from ST518 upwards, including the country buses which became ST1040-1069 (and of course the ST Bluebirds), but the conversion of the earlier Central Area buses evidently took some time as in the 1934 coding a code (1/1ST) was reserved for unconverted examples of the General type and also one (1/2ST) for unconverted examples of the Tilling type. The conversion of the 1930 country buses seems to have spread over a much longer period; I can remember the garage foreman at Grays telling me in 1947 how awful they were with only one servo, and I gained the

impression that he spoke from fairly recent experience. The Central Area ex-General T-type buses certainly all received brake conversions before they were coded (either to triple servo or Lockheed) and the Green Line coaches from T157 onwards were built with three servos, but one doubts whether the other T-type vehicles which passed through the ownership of the East Surrey, LGCS and Country Area would have been converted before disposal in 1939.

The Renowns were always triple servo, apart from LT1 in the very early days, but the original equipment of LT2-50 was not of the final design and was probably the subject of a conversion when LT1-150 were converted to 110mm bore and 6.75:1 axle ratio in 1931.

The 45 ex-LGOC T-type buses which remained with the LGOC (and Central Area) were all converted from an open rear platform to front entrance and rear emergency door, T27 in December 1930, the others between early 1933 and February 1935. In this case, as in others, the fascinating question is why the programme was not extended to other eligible candidates like the ex-ESTC examples with bodies of the same design (five of which originally came from the LGOC) after the Country Area engineering function was transferred to Chiswick in February 1935.

The first major conversion programme

Below:
T40, code 1T1. All the bodies fitted to the 45 Central Area buses of this type were converted from rear to forward entrance, T27 in 1930, the rest between 1933 and 1935. *Author*

from petrol to A165 AEC-Ricardo 8.8 litre oil engines, involving all the 170 petrol-engined crash box LT Bluebirds and 169 examples of the 1931 type, [in this analysis LT950 is included with the 1931 type] took place between September 1933 and October 1934. The engines were delivered loose from AEC against 339 reconditioned petrol engines supplied free issue from Chiswick for STL chassis. The conversion involved changing the axle ratio from 6.75:1 to 5.75:1. Twenty-four more similar conversions were undertaken in 1937 in the same way when the LTC-type coaches were built. In the latter case we know that the process began with AEC supplying the diesel engines considerably in advance of the new chassis being built. However, the 1933-34 programme involved a much larger number of engines and probably in most cases only a matter of days elapsed between an LT-type bus being brought in for conversion on overhaul and the engine removed from it being built into a new chassis at the track at AEC, having meanwhile been reconditioned at Chiswick. A study I have been able to make of the Bluebirds LT1204-1329 shows that there were peaks of conversion activity in the autumn of 1933 and the spring and autumn of 1934, these doubtless coinciding with the orders for STL253-352, 353-452 and 453-552. This programme extended over the

first three overhauls of the Plumstead Bluebirds with preselective transmission and Lockheed brakes and it appears that some migrations of this equipment took place each time between these buses and others which had previously had crash gearboxes, but that such migrations ceased once all the latter had been converted to oil engines. Hence LT964 and 1235-1238 remained petrol-engined and acquired fluid transmission and Lockheed brakes.

The omission of the Plumstead buses from the 1933-34 conversion programme is explainable on the grounds that Plumstead was not one of the garages selected for the installation of diesel facilities at that time. On conversion the Bluebirds were recoded from 5LT6 to 11LT6/4 and the 1931 type from 2LT with body codes LT3, 5 and 5/1 to 12LT with body codes LT3/1, 5/6 and 5/5.

Although the conversion of LT21 to take an A171 7.7 litre Comet Mk I oil engine in June 1935 hardly amounted to a conversion programme, it is interesting to consider the reasons why no other conversions were made with this engine. The first 11 engines in STL342-352 had run for more than a year when LT21 was converted and the engine had just been adopted as standard for new STL-type buses. Almost certainly it was not because its power — 115bhp at 200rpm — was considered inadequate. By the stan-

Below:
LT21 at King's Cross in 1946. This bus was fitted with a 7.7-litre AEC-Ricardo Comet Mk 1 engine in June 1935, the only conversion ever made using this engine. It was given an inside-stair body in March 1940, when it received the code 2/12LT3/4. *Author*

dards of a few years later it was ample and gave LT21, which retained an axle ratio of 6.75:1, quite a good performance.

A possible reason is that this conversion with a crash gearbox required an engine-driven dynamo. The only dynamo which could be accommodated on the 7.7 litre engine itself was a single 7in machine and it was not possible with this engine to arrange a drive to a chassis-mounted 8in machine alongside the gearbox. The output of a single 7in dynamo was apparently considered to be barely adequate for double-deck buses in Central Area and this was very likely the reason for which the wartime and postwar STLs were allocated to Country Area. Dynamo notwithstanding, LT21 remained a regular performer on Mortlake's Routes 9, 37 and 73 until withdrawal in 1948.

During the period under review only one order was placed by London Transport for new bodies to be fitted to existing chassis. This was early in 1935 when a contract was awarded to Weymann for 43 single-deck bodies, 31 (15090-15120) to be mounted on Reliance and 12 (15121-15132) on Regal chassis, all belonging to Country Area. Although all 43 bodies were of the same basic design the 31 which were mounted on Reliance chassis were strictly buses whereas the 12 mounted on Regal chassis

were finished to coach standards. Both varieties were 26ft long, a limitation dictated by the necessity to fit the Reliance chassis with its wheelbase of only 16ft. They were of a straightforward six-bay design in the contemporary Chiswick idiom with a door-less cab, front entrance with sliding passenger door, central rear emergency door and standard destination boxes front and rear. However, the bodies fitted to Reliances had 30 hollow-backed plywood seats of the Bluebird type, whereas those fitted to the Regals T346-357 were given seats of the new tubular aluminium type which at this stage had only been specified for the 15 double-deck bodies of the STL5/2-type and STL857. As delivered in November 1935 these bodies only had 26 seats; the seating capacity was later increased to 30 but surprisingly this was not done immediately when T346-357 were downgraded to buses, as they were on the delivery of Q189-238 some 12 months later, but not until 1939. The decision to downgrade T346-357 whilst retaining 27 4Q4s as coaches was a very questionable one as the former were much more comfortable to ride in, at least for any passenger fortunate enough to obtain a seat.

The 31 bodies on Reliance chassis, which entered service in September and October

Above:
T354, code 5T4, one of the ex-Blue Belle and Queen Line coaches rebodied in October-November 1935 with bodies generally similar to those fitted to the Reliances but with the new tubular seats. *D. W. K. Jones*

1935, in all cases but one replaced canvas-roof coach bodies with swing doors previously fitted to the same chassis. The 31st chassis was an ex-East Surrey vehicle rebuilt from a 416 which had previously carried an open-top double-deck body — a distinctly odd candidate for rebodying in 1935. The Reliances which were omitted from this rebodying programme were five of the 14 built for the National services in 1929 which still carried their original rear platform bus bodies and the nine coaches inherited from Battens, six of which continued in coach service until 1938. The Weymann body fitted to the ex-East Surrey 416 in 1935 was transferred to one of these in 1937. However, in 1938 all 31 bodies were transferred to Regal chassis which were fitted with 7.7-litre direct-injection oil engines at the same time, the resulting vehicles being coded 11T11.

The first Regal to be so converted was T396, one of the ex-East Surrey touring coaches of the 1930 batch, which was recommissioned in its new form in March 1938, the same month as most of the Regals with folding-roof bodies were sold. The rolling stock record card for this vehicle contained entries dated 15 March 1938 reading 'Coach to Bus'; 'Petrol to Oil'; 'new type Reliance body fitted', and showed the engine bore as 115mm and vehicle code as 2/7T4/1. I am, however, inclined to think that

these last two entries were erroneous. There were later undated entries of bore 106mm and code 11T11 without any note of further alterations. The original body of T396 was fitted to the chassis of R16, from which the new body had been taken, and sold with it in the October following.

The second Regal to be dealt with was T232, in August 1938. Until then T232 had carried the odd Weymann metal-framed coach body fitted in LGCS days. Here again the body removed from T232 was transferred to the Reliance chassis from which the new body was taken, R4, and sold with it in October. These transfers must have entailed more than a few minutes' work, in view of the difference in wheelbase between the Regal and Reliance chassis. It is possible that the wheelbase of these Reliance chassis was extended, perhaps by welding-in sections cut from other chassis which were being scrapped, which would have been necessary if they were to conform with the Construction & Use Regulations when fitted with bodies exceeding 26ft in length.

The remaining 1935 bodies were transferred from Reliance to Regal chassis in October and November 1938, the Reliance chassis concerned then being sold for scrap. The Regal chassis selected to receive them were all of 1931 specification with triple servo brakes as original equipment. They included 25 ex-Green Line coaches (T208, 212-16, 223, 226, 234, 236, 237, 250, 253, 255, 261, 266, 267, 271, 275, 276, 280, 283, 285, 296 and 298) and four out of the six ex-Amersham & District coaches, T359, 361, 362 and 364. Rather unexpectedly the record cards showed that Weymann bodies were also fitted to ex-Amersham T365-6 and ex-Lewis T367 in November 1938, but early the following month all three chassis were refitted with their original 1932 bodies and the 1935 Weymann bodies were mounted instead on chassis from the T207-306 batch. T365-7 were then sold, in February and March 1939.

The 31 11T11-type buses produced by this conversion programme were satisfactory if unspectacular, differing little in essential specification from the postwar Regal Mk I buses T719-768. Several were transferred to the Central Area at some stage during the remainder of their lives, which extended until 1953.

T346-357, although fitted with an extra row of seats in 1939 only a few months after the 11T11 programme, were never con-verted to oil. Several were converted to producer gas during the war (code 13T4/1) but all had been converted back to petrol by the beginning of May 1945 when they were sold to the War Department for personnel transport in Germany.

The decision to fit new bodies to Reliances in 1935 has never seemed to me to have been a good one. It should have been apparent to anyone responsible for purchasing decisions in 1935 that any AEC chassis of earlier design origin than a Regal was already hopelessly outdated, such had been the pace of progress since 1929. Investment would have been better directed in the 380 Regals which London Transport had inherited; 30 of these had bodies with swing doors which severely limited their usefulness and of the country buses, only three has front entrance bodies which conformed with the standards which had been established in Central Area. A better plan to my mind would have involved the purchase of 30 new bodies, all of which could have been mounted on 1931 speci-fication chassis numbered between T319

Below:
With the advent of the 10T10-type coaches many petrol-engined T-type coaches were downgraded to buses and in 1938 the 31 new bodies fitted to Reliance chassis in 1935 were transferred to Regal chassis which were also given 7.7-litre direct-injection oil engines and coded 11T11. Most of these like T223 seen here were formerly Green Line coaches of the 1931 series. *Author*

and 402. Enough bus bodies of Chiswick design could then have been found for all the 1930 specification non-Green Line chassis (with one to spare in fact) by appropriating the 14 bodies built for Reliances in 1929 and five in 1930. Fourteen of these were on ADC416 chassis scheduled for disposal in 1935. These bodies would, of course, have required rather more extensive rework than the 22 already fitted to Regal chassis because of the difference in wheelbase between the Reliance and Regal, but the timing would have been opportune as the conversion programme on the Central Area buses had just been completed when Country Area engineering was transferred to Chiswick in February 1935. The resulting population would then have comprised 150 rear-entrance coaches with nearside tanks, 100 front entrance coaches with bodies of the T7/1-type (those from T391/2 being used to replace the odd ones on T38 and 232), 100 doorless front entrance buses and 30 dual-purpose coaches with new bodies which could have been 27ft long. Some of the more modern displaced bodies could have been re-used, for instance to replace any substandard bodies on Tiger chassis of the TR-type. Bus bodies from other withdrawn 416s could have been fitted to any Reliances which needed to be kept pending implementation of this programme.

Following the completion of the 10T10-type coaches in 1938 it was decided to convert all the remaining petrol-engined LTs of the 1931 series with crash gearboxes (code 2LT3, 4, 5 and 5/1) to diesel, using the A180 direct-injection version of the 8.8-litre engine. This was not the special version of the engine used in the 10T10-type coaches; it used the Leyland pot type combustion system and Leyland injectors but had fan and water pump in their usual places in front of the timing case. The radiator thus has to be moved forward, as in the earlier 8.8-litre conversions, but this was the original unit retained and not a new special unit.

In this form the engine gave a bare 100bhp at 1,800rpm. This output was minimal for a bus weighing 8¼ tons; it was much less than the 130bhp rating with which the A165 (8.8 litre Comet Mk I) engine had originally been offered. It was also significantly less than the 110bhp of the A145 petrol engine it replaced. By 1939 AEC had produced a toroidal direct injection version of the 8.8 litre engine for northern users such as Sheffield, Halifax and Rochdale, for whom such a drop in power would have been completely unacceptable. This version would have given 110bhp at 1,800rpm, and moreover would have used about 5% less fuel for the work actually done than the pot-type. It would therefore

Above:
ST141, one of the Country Area buses with lowbridge bodies, in 1947, showing the raised waistrail mouldings applied to these bodies at Chiswick during and after the war. *Author*

arguably have been a better choice for these buses. However, at the time the decision to convert them was taken, London Transport was still much smitten with the pot type combustion system on its showing in STD1-100. What is surprising is that the drivers appear to have been willing to accept the reduction in available power, particularly as the axle ratio was changed to 5.75:1 which meant that the gradient ability in each gear was appreciably reduced.

The number of buses involved was 550. The programme began early in 1939 and continued into 1940. The LPTB return for 30 June 1939 shows exactly 400 buses as having been converted by that date but this is almost certainly an exaggeration. These conversions were coded 1/12LT, with body codes LT3/3, 5/7 and 5/8.

The omission of the 54 Plumstead buses with fluid transmission from this conversion programme is strange. At the time of the 1933-34 programme the oil engine was still relatively new and it is possible to understand that it may not have been desired to provide diesel fuelling and maintenance facilities at Plumstead at that time. However, the 1939-40 programme left Plumstead with the 54 preselective buses still petrol-engined whereas the 20 or 25 crash-box LTs which were needed to meet its service commitment were now perforce

oil-engined. Conversion of the 6LT Bluebirds (since 1934 the only Bluebirds remaining petrol-engined) would moreover have produced 50 buses to a virtually common specification with LT1355-1374; however, the latter remained at Hanwell. In the case of the contemporary STL conversion programme, which we shall come to shortly, it was the preselective examples which were converted and the crash-box examples which were omitted. As mentioned earlier the omission of the Plumstead buses did not prevent them from lasting for another 10 years and becoming among the last double-deck LT-type buses to survive.

The conversion of STL203-252, 254-262, 264-289, 291, 403-552 and 559-608 to oil engines was undertaken during 1939. This conversion involved substituting new engines of the A173 7.7 litre direct injection type for the original petrol engines. For these engines new flexible mountings were provided; in both these respects these buses were brought into line with STL2516-2647 whose building overlapped this conversion programme. The conversion also involved the incorporation of automatic brake adjusters, another feature used in STL2516-2647, but not automatic chassis lubrication.

The original intention with regard to the bodies of the converted vehicles seems to have been to rebuild them front and rear to

STL259, code 1/16SL17, one of the 1939 diesel conversions of former petrol-engined buses of 1933-34 vintage with fluid transmission, seen at Wembley in 1949. The body is one of 12 built in 1941 to a design originally prepared for a conversion of the bodies fitted to STL203-552 and 559-608 and using the same type of seats.
Author

the outline of the later STL bodies, including a roof-mounted front route number box, whilst leaving the central portion as it was, single panelled with no outsweep of the mudwings, except for respacing the upstairs seats. The code STL17 was raised for a body of this specification but in the event this intention was sadly abandoned in favour of re-using the original bodies with minimum alteration. This decision resulted in the rather high-at-the-front appearance of these buses as standard STL springs were used whereas these bodies were not only lighter but their centre of gravity was further aft. As converted the buses were recoded 16STL18 (STL403-552 and 559-608), 1/16STL18 (STL253-291 less 253, 263 and 290) and 2/16STL18/1 (STL203-252).

The chassis of codes 1/16STL and 2/16STL retained their Daimler gearboxes. With both types of gearbox a chassis-mounted 8in dynamo was driven by V-belts — then new — from a new pulley incorporated in the front coupling. Also retained were the original ball type selectors which were found to work satisfactorily with the flexibly-mounted engines. In slightly modified form the STL17 body design eventually appeared during the war when 12 new bodies were built in 1941 to ease the

shortage of bodies resulting from enemy action. Two of these were mounted on STL258 and 259 which thus provided an illustration of how these buses would have looked if the original plan had been adhered to. The V-belt dynamo drive which was also used on the 15STL-type chassis was later fitted to all the STL-type chassis which had originally had a chain drive within the gearbox and also to the 9T9 and 10T10-type chassis.

The last conversion programme to fall within the scope of this book was the conversion of all 8.8-litre AEC-Ricardo engines of type A165 to direct injection type A180. The vehicles involved were LT1355-1416, the 363 conversions of 1933-34 and 1937 and the 12 Country Area Godstone buses, making a total with spares of 488 engines. The pot type combustion system was again chosen bringing these engines into line with the 1939-40 conversions although none of the buses affected were recoded. The conversions to the engines involved a new cylinder block as well as pistons, cylinder heads, injectors and alterations to the fuel injection pump. This programme was sanctioned in October 1939. Conversions began in 1940 and were completed in 1943.

12: London Transport Innovation: the TF, CR and RT Types

During the years 1937, 1938 and 1939 London Transport introduced three entirely new types of vehicle, two of which were commissioned from Leyland and one from AEC. The two which were commissioned from Leyland, the TF and CR-types, both broke new ground in respect of chassis layout, the TF having the engine amidships under the floor with the cylinders horizontal and the CR-type having it at the rear, where it was mounted longitudinally with the cylinders upright.

In 1937 the only British bus chassis design which had diverged with any success from the formula of having the engine between the frames at the front with the cylinders vertical had been the AEC Q-type. The past tense is chosen because the last examples produced were delivered in 1937, but London Transport's support for the single-deck version — its 232 vehicles represented about three quarters of the total produced

— had ensured some success for this unorthodox model. In planning these new designs London Transport again demonstrated its readiness to accept single-deckers of unconventional concept but not double-deckers. This is not to say that the RT-type was lacking in innovative features: it was a totally new design, literally from the wheels up, but as a concept it was evolutionary, not revolutionary.

The preliminary discussions with Leyland which led to the building of the first TF chassis probably began about the beginning of 1937 or the end of 1936, possibly even before those preceding the order for STD1-100. TF1 actually had an earlier chassis number — 11176 — than the latter, although this was next to that of a TD4c demonstration model and may not be a valid indicator of production date for an experimental chassis. However, TF1 complete with a Leyland-built body was licensed

Below:
The licensing shop at Chiswick in June 1939 showing RT1, a TF-type coach and an assortment of overhauled buses. *LT U29877*

in September 1937, only two months after the last 10 Titans entered service at Hendon. No LPTB sanction number for TF1 is known but its relatively late body number, 18075, suggests that it may not have passed into London Transport ownership until some time the following year.

London Transport experience with the Q-type clearly influenced the design of TF1 in several ways. Things which it was desired to avoid included an engine which protruded above floor level — dictating a need for inward-facing longitudinal seats which were considered inappropriate for a coach — and a weight distribution in which the centre of gravity was appreciably offset from the longitudinal centre line. This last had given rise in the Q-type to a need for the four springs all to be different; even then there were difficulties in ensuring that the vehicles stood level both empty and fully laden, and the tyres had to be rated for the load carried by the most heavily laden wheel. In the TF layout the entire driveline was on the chassis centreline and the weight of the cylinder block on the offside was counterbalanced by the fuel tank on the nearside. The axle employed an overhead worm drive with a ratio of 5.4:1. In TF1 single tyres were used all round, as they had been in the Q-type; significantly, however, they were a size smaller, at 9.75×20. In TF2-88 the weight distribution was altered and twin rear tyres were used, the size now being 9.00×20 as in the 10T10-type. The

wheelbase remained at 18ft 6in, the same as the Q-type in its standard single-deck form.

Transmission was by fluid flywheel and AEC D132 preselective gearbox. Here London Transport showed no willingness to accept a standard Leyland crash gearbox transmission and in this matter the experience with Q1 was probably decisive. Both brakes and gearbox were operated by compressed air; the gearbox, being of the usual type with an internal spring, required an external air cylinder to disengage the gears. This meant that if the vehicle was left in gear overnight it might not be possible to disengage gear until air pressure had been built up, but this did not prevent the engine being started (as the fluid flywheel allowed this) and the compressor was engine driven. Although this might be thought to have been a safety hazard in garages, I have never heard that any problems ever arose in practice. Nevertheless, this arrangement was not adopted in the RT-type. In TF1 the gears were originally selected electromagnetically from a switch below the steering wheel, but this, as in Q188, was later replaced by a standard AEC ball-type selector, floor mounted on the driver's left, but placed further forward than usual to facilitate access from the saloon and inclined backwards. The air pressure brakes used front cylinders mounted on the kingpins — an arrangement which had been used on Q188, STL757 and 758 and was to be used on the RT-type. It meant that the

Below:
TF1 as first delivered, in Green Line service working from Tunbridge Wells on Eccleston Bridge, Victoria, in 1938.
D. W. K. Jones

axle had to be of the design used by Leyland up to the TD5 and TS8 models, in which the wheel load was transmitted through a roller thrust bearing surrounding the king pin, as the latter had to be hollow.

The engine was a special version of the Leyland 8.6-litre overhead-camshaft direct injection unit used in the STD-type, a design with which (as we have seen) London Transport was greatly taken at the time. The crankcase and sump had to be redesigned to allow the engine to lie on its side and the fuel injection pump was situated beneath the cylinder head. The engine was carried in a Metalastik two-point mounting similar to that used in the RT and 15STL-types, with the rear mounting encasing the fluid flywheel — this being made possible by the use of a separate gearbox. The use of this system on TF1 may, in fact, have been its first application. From the front of the crankshaft a rubber jointed shaft continued forward to the cooling fan which with the radiator was in front of the axle.

Although the wheelbase was longer, the axles were both in pretty much the positions they would have occupied in an orthodox vehicle. No attempt was made to cater for an entrance in front of the front axle; coaches would carry a conductor for as far as could be seen into the future and a sliding door was wanted, which meant that it had to be behind the front wheel. Over the nearside front wheel was a forward facing double seat which provided an incomparable vantage point. The floor was slightly higher than in the 10T10-type and there were three internal steps instead of two. The seating capacity was 34 in the Green Line versions (TF1 and 13-88) all facing forward; the Park Royal sightseeing coaches TF2-13, which had an offside instead of a rear emergency door, seated 33.

As first built TF1 had a raised driving position which went with a half-canopy construction and resulted in a rather strange appearance. In 1940 — at about the time of the evacuation from Dunkirk — this was altered to a more orthodox cab with a full-width canopy incorporating a standard destination box. However, TF1 was destined not to see a great deal of service before the Green Line services were discontinued for the duration of the war at the end of which it was sold. It was then bought by a coach operator in Lewisham from whom it was one of the vehicles hired by London Transport under its get-you-home plan in 1946-47.

A production batch of 87 TF-type coaches, TF2-88, ordered against sanction G305 was delivered in 1939 with bodies numbered 1-87 beginning a new series. Of TF2-13, the sightseeing coaches with Park Royal 'greenhouse' bodies (code 2TF3), sadly all but TF9 were destroyed in the air raid on Bull Yard, Peckham in October 1940. TF14-88 received straightforward Chiswick-built 34-seat bodies (code 2TF2) for use on the Green Line services on which they replaced the last petrol-engined Regals of the T207-306 series at Luton, St Albans, Grays and Dorking in the summer of 1939. After serving as ambulances during the war they resumed the Green Line services at these garages on their reintroduction and they remained in service until 1952-53.

The next of London Transport's special designs to appear was the first rear-engined Leyland Cub, CR1, which entered Country Area service in January 1938. The 20-seat Chiswick-built body, numbered 18001 in a series which had been left blank, bore a certain family resemblance to the TF-type. The same thinking was apparent in that the driver entered via the saloon, the (sliding) passenger door was behind the front wheel and a full-fronted treatment was not attempted. However, a full-width canopy with standard destination box was fitted from the start.

The chassis of CR1 was received at Chiswick on 16 October 1937. It became

London Transport property on sanction G280 on 30 December and the body was mounted the next day. It had a 4.4-litre direct-injection engine of the type fitted to the Country Area Cubs. This was mounted longitudinally on the rear overhang and drove forward to a special constant mesh gearbox through the hollow wormshaft of the final drive, which was sandwiched between the engine and the gearbox. The rear axle was of the de Dion type, allowing the use of twin rear tyres. After a few weeks at St Albans CR1 was allocated to Windsor, where C76 could stand in for it during the initial period when teething troubles had to be expected.

Forty-eight further buses included in sanction G305 were ordered in 1939 to replace the surviving Central Area Dennis Darts and Country Area Bedfords. These buses, CR2-49, were not completed until after the outbreak of war and when completed were put into store. They had engines of the indirect-injection type as used in the Central Area Cubs including five, CR12-16, which were painted green. The Chiswick-built bodies (numbered 224-271) were of a modified design in which the door was moved to a position immediately behind the front wheel (without altering the seating capacity) and as in the production TF-type coaches a straight waistline was adopted. Except for CR18, which was destroyed in the air raid on Bull Yard, CR2-49 remained in store until the end of the war when they were brought into service as rush-hour reliefs with conductors. Later they were moved to Country Area where they did not completely displace the surviving front-engined Cubs. Both types were replaced by GS-type front-engined 26-seaters in 1953.

The last and best known of the new vehicle designs commissioned by London Transport before the war was the RT-type from AEC. Although of orthodox layout, this was a completely new design of double-decker. The frame was a new design, parallel at the front and slightly narrower at the rear to allow the use of wider rims for the twin rear wheels. All the major units were new. The rear axle had a larger (8in centres) worm gear in the offset differential. The gearbox, type D140, was a new design with an internal air cylinder to apply the gears instead of the previous spring. The engine was also a new design, with increased cylinder centres and gear type timing case. In the first build of the chassis in 1938 the engine used was one of the prototype A182 units of 115mm bore and 142mm stroke (which we have met in STL2513-2515) but before it became RT1 with its new purpose-designed body in March 1939 it received a new engine of 120mm bore, the first 9.6-litre unit, type A185. With the Leyland pot type combustion system which London Transport favoured at that time this was rated at 108bhp at 1,800rpm, the same power as the 7.7-litre

Comet Mk III engine gave at 2,000rpm. The axle ratio chosen, 5.167:1, exactly compensated for the lower engine speed compared with the 5.75:1 used in the STL-type.

The engine was mounted in a two-point Metalastik 'floating power' suspension, the rear mounting encasing the fluid flywheel. The latter was still of the 16in size, as used in the STL-type.

The front axle was also a new design with the operating cylinders for the brakes mounted on the kingpins. Both brakes and gearbox were actuated by a compressed air system, fed at this stage by an engine-driven rotary compressor (later a transmission-driven reciprocating compressor was substituted); this resulted in a transformation of the pedal effort needed for braking and changing gear. The radiator was a new design, low and flat, carried on an inward extension of the front spring anchor pins. So compact were the new timing case and mounting arrangements that the effective bonnet length was only 1⅜in more than that of a Regent with petrol or 7.7-litre oil engine.

The gear selector was moved to a position beneath the steering wheel on the driver's left; it was still of the staggered gate type but working in a horizontal plane. In this position it had the advantage of not being affected by the movement of the engine on its soft rubber mounting. Automatic brake adjusters and automatic chassis lubrication were included in the specification. Interestingly, the fuel tank was mounted on the nearside, a throwback to the General ST-type.

The chassis of RT1 was built as an experimental joint venture between London Transport and AEC. It was delivered to Chiswick on 23 May 1938 and having been purchased on a special sanction, G316, became London Transport property on 30 June. It was then fitted with a body from a scrapped ex-independent Leyland Titan (TD118) and, numbered ST1140, was placed in service at Hanwell from the middle of July until the end of the year. The ex-TD body was then removed and scrapped and the chassis was returned to AEC for modifications to suit its future guise as RT1. These included fitting the new engine and removal of the frame extensions behind the rear spring shackles.

The new body, 18246, was mounted on 27 March 1939. To carry the platform loads unsupported by the chassis, all-metal construction was adopted for the first time in a Chiswick-built body. With its four-bay design the RT body was a striking-looking artefact by the standards of the time, achieving a much cleaner and smoother effect than the STL body, the last examples of which had yet to be built. As in the 10T10 and TF bodies the winding half-drop windows were fitted in rubber-glazed pans with radiused corners and the roof was fully double-skinned, including the domes. Compared with the later standard STL-type

bodies the only alteration in the seating was that the two single seats upstairs were now replaced by one double seat. The lower bonnet line allowed the use of a straight lower edge to the front bulkhead windows in the lower saloon; however, the cab side window and windscreen both drooped towards the corner — a detail which was repeated in the bodies of RT2-151 although abandoned in postwar bodies. The cab had a forward-sliding door which could be left open in warm weather — something which could not be done with the hinged door of the 10T10.

The single-line blind for the destination was reduced in width to match the deeper blind for the intermediate points. The route number box was situated in the roof dome, happily at the front but most unhappily, also at the rear where it stood out like the proverbial sore thumb. This was one of very few visually unpleasing details of the RT body and it was wisely abandoned in postwar bodies which had a rear display of only two blinds. As in the 10T10-type the (nearside) front wing was carried on the body.

Although the detailed design of the RT body achieved a much cleaner effect than the STL, its overall balance as a composition was not to my eye as good: this was because the curvature of the front was increased whereas that of the rear was reduced — to nothing in fact, the line of the

back falling vertically from the upper deck waistrail.

Perhaps the most remarkable thing of all about the RT-type was that all this was achieved almost without increase on the weight of the STLs built at Chiswick in 1936-38. The licensing weight of RT1 with its metal-framed body came out at 6tons 15cwt 2qr, which forced the substitution of a single seat for a double at the top of the stairs to comply with the permitted gross weight limit of 10ton 10cwt; it ran as a 55-seater throughout its service life from 17 June 1939, when it was sent to Chelverton Road until October 1945 when it was withdrawn for the body to be transferred to RT19. The latter had then just been converted at AEC to the postwar 3RT specification, with a new version of the 9.6-litre engine with toroidal DI combustion system (A204), 18in diameter fluid flywheel, a new gearbox (D150) with V-belt driven dynamo and reciprocating compressor and, of course, truncated side-members.

A further 150 buses, RT2-151, were ordered on Sanction G325 which included STL2631-2647 and CR2-49 and was probably raised early in 1939. Coded 2RT2 with body numbers 280-429, RT2-151 represented a certain technical retreat compared with RT1 insofar as they had full length chassis frames and the bodies were of the metallised composite construction used for the Chiswick-built 10T10 and TF bodies,

with hardwood pillars. Neither of these changes was visible to passengers, however, and the licensing weight came down to 6ton 12cwt — exactly the same as the 1936-38 Chiswick-built STLs — allowing the inclusion of 56 seats.

Had it not been for the outbreak of war in September 1939 the order would have been larger. The number originally proposed was 338, which would have made it possible to replace all the remaining buses still running in Central Area with outside stairs. Construction of the 150 bodies at Chiswick followed on from CR2-49 between December 1939 and May 1940; the battle of Dunkirk was raging when the last few were being completed. Understandably, the delivery of the chassis from AEC was more protracted and although the first of these buses entered service in January 1940 the last, RT151, did not do so until January 1942. The first buses completed were sent to join RT1 at Chelverton Road but many of those delivered later ran from the new garage at Gillingham Street, Victoria for much of the war, only moving to Putney High Street towards its end.

Early in the service life of the RT-type trouble was experienced with the rotary compressor. These were also the early days of compressed air systems on buses and the original design of the RT chassis incorporated a single drive from the timing case via a universal jointed shaft on the offside of the engine to a frame-mounted compressor and

Below:
CR1 in Broadway, Westminster, for the purpose of demonstration to the LPTB chief officers, January 1938. The prominent rear hub of these vehicles housed the outboard universal joint of the de Dion rear axle. *D. W. K. Jones*

Above:
**RT1, an official photograph
thought to be in Bushey Park,
April 1939. Note the staircase
window.** *LT21076*

dynamo under the saloon floor. The compressor thus ran at dynamo speed, about one-and-a-half times engine speed, unlike the vacuum exhauster used in the STL-type which was incorporated in the drive to the fuel pump and so ran at half engine speed. This was presumably similar to the arrangement which had been used in STL757, 758 and Q188 but these, like RT1, may have had a German Bosch compressor which obviously ceased to be available on the outbreak of war. The 2RTs had a Clayton Dewandre compressor with which the troubles originally experienced were so severe as to necessitate the withdrawal from service of all the RT-type buses which were then running for a period in 1940. One of the last chassis, RT143, was placed in traffic with a reciprocating compressor driven by V-belts from the front of the gearbox which (such had been the confidence in the original arrangements) had lacked provision for either dynamo or compressor drive as first designed. RT143 was followed in 1943-44 by 49 similar conversions; coded 1/2RT2/1, these retained the original drive to the

dynamo from the engine timing case. Design changes to the rotary compressor had meanwhile increased its service life to an average of 20,000 miles — six months running — and the remaining buses continued thus until they were made the subject of a conversion programme in 1949-50 in which both dynamo and compressor were belt driven from the front of the gearbox — the arrangement used in RT19 and the postwar 3RTs. These later conversions were coded 3/2RT2/2.

The chassis of RT1 was dismantled at Chiswick in September 1946. Its body was later transferred from RT19 to RT1420 whose original Cravens body had been damaged beyond economical repair in an accident and this is the combination which survives preserved in the guise of RT1 today. RT19 was then mounted with a former Tilling ST body which had previously been fitted to a postwar 3RT chassis for training purposes during the shortage of bodies in the late 1940s.

Except for RT97 (used for yet another attempt as a double-deck coach) and a couple of casualties, the 2RTs worked until 1955, latterly from Chelverton Road and the former tram depot at New Cross. After this seven of them were painted green and ran from Hertford until a weak bridge on one route was replaced in August 1957. Their weight, then given as 6ton 15cwt, was still 15cwt less than that of the postwar 3RTs. Happily a 2RT has been preserved.

RT1-151 were the precursors of a whole new generation of London buses, destined to be more numerous even than the famous B-type. Their position in history is thus different from that of STL2516-2647, which represented the final development of the AEC Regent from its original 1929 concept just as Birmingham's TD6s represented the final development of Rackham's original Titan. Even with their wheel discs, deep radiators, flexibly-mounted direct-injection engines, self-adjusting brakes and automatic chassis lubrication, STL2516-2647 were patently AEC Regents and still had much in common with ST1139, including the frame width and the basic driver's structure. A consequence of the 1939-45 war was that production of both the Regent and Regal, in a form even closer to the original

1929 concept with solid-mounted 7.7-litre engines and crash gearboxes, was resumed for some two years after its end; during this period London Transport had some of both types. During the war they also had 34 Regents of similarly basic specification which AEC were allowed to build in 1941 from parts which were already on hand.

The outbreak of war in September 1939 found London Transport very well prepared. The vigorous policy of replacement of nonstandard types pursued since 1933 had achieved a position where the service fleet included only four types of double-decker, four types of full-size single-decker (including coaches), and two types of small one-man bus, in addition to which there were the prototype RT1 and RT2-151 on order. The war marked the end of an era in Europe; it was to change a great deal in the lives of everyone in Britain and it is sad to have to end by recording that the 46 STL bodies built in 1941 and 1942 were the last ever to be built in the factory at Chiswick. Although the last 20 broke new ground in being of the lowbridge type, even these conformed with the Chiswick STL tradition in having doorless cabs and bulb horns.

Below:
The postwar world; scene at King's Cross (still London & North Eastern Railway) early in 1947. Seen here are a CR with grey roof on rush-hour relief, two 2RTs and two STLs, both pairs in different liveries, as well as 27ft and 30ft long trolleybuses. *LT 17994*

Appendices

1 LGOC rolling stock purchase sanctions 1929-33 and LPTB rolling stock purchase sanctions 1933-39.
2 Analysis of London Transport bus and coach fleets at 30 June 1936, 1937, 1938 and 1939, as published in LPTB Annual Reports.
3 ST type chassis codes, specifications and corresponding body codes.
4 T type chassis codes, specifications and corresponding body codes.
5 LT type chassis codes, specifications and corresponding body codes.
6 STL type chassis codes, specifications and corresponding body codes.
7 Q, C, STD, LTC, TF, CR, and RT type specifications and codes.

Key to abbreviations used

Engines (All six-cylinder)

A140	AEC	100mm × 130mm	petrol
A145	AEC	110mm × 130mm	petrol
A161	AEC	115mm × 142mm	AEC-Ricardo (original type) oil
A165	AEC	115mm × 142mm	AEC-Ricardo (1932 and later) oil
A167	AEC	110mm × 130mm	Q-type petrol
A170	AEC	106mm*× 146mm	Q-type AEC-Ricardo oil
A171	AEC	106mm*× 146mm	AEC-Ricardo oil (orthodox)
A173	AEC	105mm × 146mm	toroidal DI oil
A180	AEC	115mm × 142mm	direct-injection oil
A182	AEC	115mm × 142mm	direct-injection oil (new type)
A185	AEC	120mm × 142mm	direct-injection oil (new type)

*105mm for later engines with Comet Mk III combustion system

6LW	Gardner	4¼in × 6in	direct-injection oil
0-8.6	Leyland	4½in × 5½in	direct-injection oil
CP	Leyland	3⅜in × 5in	side-valve petrol
CO	Leyland	3⅜in × 5in	direct-injection oil
ZP	Leyland	3½in × 5in	overhead-valve petrol
ZO	Leyland	3½in × 5in	indirect-injection oil

Gearboxes

D124	AEC	4-speed crash
D128	Daimler	4-speed preselective
D129	Daimler	4-speed preselective Q-type
D132	AEC	4-speed preselective
D133	AEC	4-speed preselective Q-type
D140	AEC	4-speed air-operated preselective
4-sp	Leyland	4-speed crash with helical 3rd speed
TC	Leyland	Gearless transmission (torque converter)

Rear Axles

SF	semi-floating
FF	fully floating
dD	de Dion

Brakes

SM	servo-assisted mechanical
3S	triple servo
SH	servo-assisted hydraulic

Fuel tank position

OS	offside
NS	nearside
ON	offside and nearside

Bodies

b	body
bb	bodies
d-box	destination box
dd	double-deck
fl-trap	floortrap
s	seat(s)
sd	single-deck
sp	spare
wb	wheelbase
AWC	All-weather coach, ie one with sliding or folding roof
BRCW	Birmingham Railway Carriage & Wagon Co Ltd
MCCW	Metropolitan-Cammell Carriage & Wagon Co Ltd
O/A	overall

Appendix 1: LGOC Vehicle Purchase Sanctions 1929-33

No	Authorisation	Bonnet Numbers	Remarks	Body Numbers
24/918	6 CC		Later reduced to 4	10478-10493
	6 CB		Later reduced to 3	
	2 Renown 664		Later cancelled	
	1 Regent chassis	ST517	ST169 actually used	
	1 Regent	ST1		
953	50 Regal	T1-50	T38 used for coach	10228-10277
977	50 Renown 663	LT1-50	b10185 used for LT1	10278-10326
978	50 Renown 664	LT1001-1050		10327-10376*
979	300 Regent	ST2-301	9spbb (10955-10963)	10377-10476*, 10503-10702
981	1 Regent (ESTC)	(ST1139)		10954
995	15 Regent (NOTC)	ST502-516		11149-11163
996	100 Regal	T51-149, 155		11004-11103
1003	1 Regal	T156	Replacement for T38	
1010	200 Regent	ST302-501		11335-11534
1011	100 Renown 663	LT51-150	spbb12005-9 (24/1033)	11169-11268
	5 Regal	T150-154		(8856-8860)
1025	50 Regal	T157-206		11285-11334
1032	300 Regal	ST518-817	15spbb b 12309 cancelled	12010-12308, 12340-12354
1033	100 Renown 663	LT151-250	8spbb	11895-12004
1034	100 Regal	T207-306		11795-11894
1038	250 Renown 663	LT251-500	7spbb	11545-11794

No	Authorisation	Bonnet Numbers	Remarks	Body Numbers
1039	1 spare T, 1 spare LTL body		b11543 later cancelled	11543/4
1046	3 Daimler CH6	DST1-3		12310-2
1047	15 Regent (O'gd)	ST822-836		12313-12327
1051	4 Regent (NOTC)	ST818-821		12920-12923
1055	28 Regent (ESTC)	(ST1040-4/7-69)		12359-12386
1056	4 Regent (ESTC)	(ST1085-1088)	ex-Autocar	12355-12358
1064	50 Renown 664	LT1052-1101	2spbb	12387-12438
1069	450 Renown 663	LT501-950	13spbb	12439-12901
1089	3 Regal (ESTC)	(T380-382)		13055/84/6
1094	100 Renown 664	LT1102-1201	3spbb	129217-13029
1115	250 Renown 663	LT951-99/1204-1404	8spbb	13087-13344
?	23 Regent (LGCS)	(ST1032 (1032-9/1070-84)		13441-13465
	2 Renown 664 (LGCS)	(LT1427, 1428)		
1141	22 Renown 663	LT1405-1426		13419-13440
1143	102 Regent (Tlg)	STL51-153	Last 22 cancelled	
	12 Regal (Tlg)	T307-318		
1150	50 Regent	STL1-50		13470-13519
1154	1 Q sd	Q1		13466
1158	1 spare Tilling T, 4 spare Tilling STL bodies			
1159	100 Regent	STL153-252		13547-13650
1169	100 Regent	STL253-352	89 oil engines for LT	13685-13787

*The numbers originally intended for these two batches were 10328-10377 and 10378-10477.

LPTB Vehicle Purchase Sanctions 1933-39

No	Authorisation	Bonnet Numbers	Remarks	Body Numbers
E1	2 Q dd	(Q4,5)		
E2	12 Regent	(STL1044-1055)		
D10	2 Q dd	Q2, 3		14698/9
D11	100 Regent	STL353-452	100 oil engines for LT	14156-14259
D15	100 Regent	STL453-552	100 oil engines for LT	14356-14458
D20	1 Leyland Cub	C1		14756
D26	200 Regent	STL559-758	50 oil engines for LT	14492-14697
E20	85 Regent	STL959-1043		14812-14896
E24	74 Leyland Cub	C2-74		14916-14989
E25	100 Q sd	Q6-105		14990-15089
E26	43 new bodies (31 R, 12 T)			15090-15132
DA41	200 Regent	STL759-958		15133-15338
H52	4 Regent	STL1056-1059		15512-15515
DA51	4 Regent	STL1260-1263	Chassis only, 15ft 6½in wb	
DA54	200 Regent	STL1060-1259		15576-15781
H61	80 Q sd	Q106-185		16151-16230
H62	20 Leyland Cub	C77-96		16131-16150
H63	1 Q dd	Q188		16130
H72	2 Leyland Cub	C97, 98		16254/5
	2 Q sd	Q186, 187		16256/7
H75	200 Regent	STL1264-1463		16280-16485
H76	50 Regent	STL1464-1513		16670-16719
H87	50 Regal	T403-452		16620-16669
	50 Q sd	Q189-238		16730-16779
H89	500 Regent	STL1514-2013		16834-17333
H90	8 Leyland Cub	C106-113		16722-16729
G261	100 Leyland TD4	STD1-100		17335-17434
G276	175 Regent	STL2014-2188		17435-17609
G280	327 Regent	STL2189-2515		17634-17690
	150 Regal	T453-602		18096-18245
	1 Leyland CR	CR1		(18001)
?	1 Leyland TF	TF1		(18075)
?	12 spare STL bodies			18076-18087
G283	24 Renown 663	LTC1-24	24 oil engines for LT	17610-17633
G305	116 Regal	T603-718		18247-18365
	87 Leyland TF	TF2-88		1-87
	115 Regent	STL2516-2630		88-202
G316	1 RT	RT1		18246
G325	17 Regent	STL2631-2647		207-223
	48 Leyland CR	CR2-49		224-271
	150 RT	RT2-151		280-429

Appendix 2: Breakdown of London Transport Bus and Coach Fleet as given in Annual Reports ostensibly at dates shown

Type	Fuel	Seats	30 June 1936			30 June 1937			30 June 1938			30 June 1939		
			Central Buses	Country Buses	Coaches	Central Buses	Country Buses	Coaches	Central Buses	Country Buses	Coaches	Central Buses	Country Buses	Coaches
NS	Petrol	50-52	1,032			366								
LS	Petrol	56	11											
ST	Petrol	48-54	1,009	128		1,011	126		1,011	126		1,011	126	
LT	Petrol	54-60	781	1		769	1		757	1		353	1	
	Oil	56-60	445			455			467			869		
	Petrol	32-35	199	2	1	199	2	1	190	2	1	192		25
T	Petrol	26-32	60	27	293	60	39	281	60	39	208+8ctl	54	24	
	Oil	30-34			12			53		1	160	5	57	287
STL	Petrol	50-60	571			572			574			424		
	Oil	48-56	720	101		1344	151		1760	151		1,983	169	
STF	Oil	56	1			1								
Q	Petrol	55	2	2			4			4			4	
	Petrol	37		1			1			1			1	
	Oil	51								1			1	
	Oil	32-37	53	100		53	102	77	53	102	77	57	124	51
C	Oil	20	23	74		23	74		23	74		23	73	
	Petrol	20		1			1	8		1	8		1	8
R	Petrol	26-32		39	6		39	6		33				
BD	Petrol	20		19			19			8			8	
DA	Petrol	17-18	44			44			37			32		
DC	Petrol	20-25		1			3							
DL	Petrol	47-53	33			33								
DT	Petrol			4	5		4	5						
GF	Petrol	23-32		53	87		1	14						
MS	Petrol	20		8	2		8	2						
TC	Petrol	62	3			3								
TD	Petrol	48-56	112	52		112	25		111	20		35	14	
	Oil	50-56	9			9			9					
	Petrol	25-30		2	19		2	19		2				
TR	Petrol	26-32		3	37		3	39		5	3			
Misc	Petrol	20-32		9	6		6	6						
STD	Oil	55-56				93			100			100		
TF	Oil	34									1			58+12ctl
CR	Oil	20								1			1	
			5,108	627	468	5,147	611	511	5152	572	466	5,138	604	465

Appendix 3: ST type. Chassis codes, specifications and related body codes

Chassis Code	Wheelbase	Overall Length	Engine	Gearbox	Rear Axle	Brakes	Fuel Tank Position	Bonnet Numbers	Dates	Related Body Code	Description	Notes
1ST						3S	NS	ST1-836 with exceptions	1934-	ST1	b10493 with square cab only	later converted to round cab (ST1/1)
1/1ST						SM	NS		1934 only	ST1/1	1930 bb with square backed seats	
										ST2	1931bb with round backed seats	
										ST2/1	10bb with d-box in cab canopy	
										ST3	MCW all-metal (b11535)	
										ST6	50-seat b 12037 only	
										ST6/1	do. with d-box in cab canopy	
2/1ST						SM	NS	ST107/11/6/29/32/5/43/52/9	1935-	ST9	ST1/1-type	Country Area with small d-box
						3S	NS	ST818-21/33/4/1040-50/2-69	1935-	ST9	ST2-type	do. excl ST819/20 to Cent. Area 1937
						SM	OS	ST1085-8, 1091-1132	1935-	ST9	Ransomes ex-Autocar & ESTC	do. square cab, fixed f-windows
	15ft 6½in	25ft	A140	D124	6¼ SF	SM	OS	ST1133-8	1935-	ST9	Short Bros inside stairs 6-bay	do. ex-Lewis
						SM	OS	ST1139	1935-	ST9	Short Bros outside stair 6-bay	do. ex-ESTC/AEC demonstrator
3/1ST						SM	NS	ST136/40/1/57/62/3	1935-	ST9/1	Short Bros lowbridge 6-bay	
						SM	OS	ST1089/90	1935-		Short Bros lowbridge 6-bay	
2ST						3S	OS	ST837-1027	1934-	ST7	Tilling outside-stair 6-bay	
1/2ST						SM	OS		1934			
2/2ST						3S	NS	ST1028	1934-	ST8	Birch outside-stair 5-bay	
3/2ST						3S	OS	ST1029	1934-	ST8/1	Dodson outside-stair 6-bay	
4/2ST						3S	OS	ST1030	1934-	ST8/2	Dodson outside-stair 6-bay	
5/2ST						3S	OS	ST1031	1934-	ST8/3	Birch outside-stair 5-bay	
3ST						3S	NS	ST1032-9, 1070-84	1935-	ST4	Bluebird type corner staircase	

Appendix 4: T Type Chassis codes, specifications and related body codes

Chassis Code	Wheelbase	Overall Length	Engine	Gearbox	Rear Axle	Brakes	Fuel Tank Position	Vehicles to which applicable	Dates	Related Body Code	Description	Notes
1T	17ft 0in	26ft 0in*	A140	D124	5¾ SF	3S	OS	T1-50 and 156 with exceptions	1934-	T1	30-seat front entrance	
1/1T	17ft 0in	26ft 0in	A140	D124	5¾ SF	SH	OS		1934-	T1		
2/1T	17ft 0in	26ft 0in	A145	D124	6¼ SF	3S	OS		1934-	T1		
3/1T	17ft 0in	26ft 0in	A140	D124	6¼ SF	SH	OS		1934-	T1		
4/1T	17ft 0in	26ft 0in	A140	D124	6¼ SF	SM	OS	T369	1935-9	T6	29-seat open rear platform	to 1/7T7/1, 1939
4/1T	17ft 0in	26ft 0in	A145	D124	6¼ SF	3S	OS	T370	1935-6	T6	30-seat rear entrance	spare Tilling body (4/1T3) 1936-9
4/1T	17ft 0in	26ft 0in	A145	D124	6¼ SF	SM	OS	T371	1935-	T6	30-seat front entrance	
4/1T	17ft 0in	26ft 0in	A145	D124	6¼ SF	SM	OS	T372-9, 383-90	1935-	T6	29-seat open rear platform	Hall Lewis bodies ex-ESTC
4/1T	17ft 0in	27ft 0in	A145	D124	6¼ SF	3S	OS	T380-2	1935-	T6	30-seat front entrance	Weymann bodies ex-ESTC
5/1T	17ft 0in	26ft 0in	A145	D124	6¼ SF	SM	OS	T15, 21, 25, 26, 35	1935-	T1/1	29-seat open rear platform	Chiswick bodies ex-ESTC
2T	17ft 0in	26ft 0in	A145	D124	6¼ SF	3S	OS	T43	1934-	T2	30-seat front entrance	Code applied in error
3T	17ft 0in	26ft 0in	A145	D124	5¾ SF†	SH	OS	T309-318	1934-	T3	30-seat front entrance (Tilling)	Also T307/8 from later 1934
4T	17ft 0in	26ft 0in	A145	D128	5¾ SF	SH	OS	T307/8	1934	T3	30-seat front entrance (Tilling)	To 3T3, 5/ and 9/34
5T	17ft 0in	26ft 0in	A145	D124	6¼ SF	SH	OS	T346-357	1935-	T4	26-seat Weymann (LPTB design)	30 seats 1939-
6T	not used											
7T	17ft 0in	26ft 0in	A145	D124	6¼ SF	SM	OS	T38	1935-	T7	28-seat rear swing door	
7T	17ft 0in	26ft 0in	A145	D124	6¼ SF	SM	NS	T 51-149, 155	1935-	T7	27-seat recessed rear door	T120 to 1/7T7/1, 1945
7T	17ft 0in	26ft 0in	A145	D124	6¼ SF	3S	NS	T157-206	1935-	T7	27-seat recessed rear door	
1/7T	17ft 0in	26ft 0in	A145	D124	6¼ SF	3S	OS	T207-306, 391/2 less 216, 232, 268, 274, 305	1935-	T7/1	30-seat front sliding door	
												26 converted to 11T11, 1938
	17ft 0in	26ft 9in**	A145	D124	6¼ SF	3S	OS	T232	1935-	T7/2	do; 1933 Weymann body	
2/7T	17ft 0in	26ft 4in**	A161	D124	6¼ SF	3S	OS	T216, 274, 305	1935-	T7/1	Chiswick design	T216 to 11T11 1938
8T	17ft 0in	27ft 0in	A140	D124	6¼ SF	SM	OS	T150-154	1935-	T8	Hoyal folding-roof 2 swing doors	
	17ft 0in	27ft 0in	A140	D124	6¼ SF	3S	OS	T319-324, 399-402	1935-	T8/1	Park Royal AWC front swing door	
	17ft 0in	27ft 0in	A140	D124	6¼ SF	SM	OS	T393-398	1935-	T8/2	Hall Lewis AWC 2 swing doors	T396 to 11T11 3/38
1/8T	17ft 0in	27ft 0in	A140	D124	6¼ SF	3S	OS	T359/61/2/4-6	1935-	T8/3	Strachan 32s rear sliding door	T359/61/2/4 to 11T11 10/38
not coded	17ft 0in	27ft 0in	A140	D124	6¼ SF	SM	OS	T360/3			Harrington 32s swing doors	
	17ft 0in	27ft 0in	A140	D124	6¼ SF	SM	OS	T358			Metcalfe 31s rear sliding door	
	17ft 0in	27ft 0in	A140	D124	6¼ SF	SM	OS	T367/8			Harrington 32s rear sliding door	
9T	17ft 6in	27ft 6in	A171	D132	5⅕ FF	SH	OS	T403-452	1936-	T9	30-seat Weymann	LPTB design
10T	17ft 6in	27ft 6in	A180	D124	5⅕ FF	SH	OS	T453-577	1938-	T10	30-seat Chiswick	LPTB design
	17ft 6in	27ft 6in	A180	D124	5⅕ FF	SH	OS	T603-718	1939-	T10/1	34-seat Chiswick	LPTB design
1/10T	17ft 6in	27ft 6in	A180	D124	6¼ FF	SH	OS	T578-602	1938-	T10	30-seat Chiswick	LPTB design
11T	17ft 0in	26ft 0in	A173	D124	5⅕ SF	3S	OS	T208/12-16/23/6/32/4 236/7/50/3/5/61/3/6 267/71/5/6/80/3/96/8 359/61/2/4/96	1938-	T11	30-seat Weymann ex-R-type	LPTB design

*T10 only, 25ft 6in   †FF in one case   **Approximate

Appendix 5: LT type Chassis codes, specifications and related body codes

Chassis Code	Wheelbase	Overall Length	Engine	Gearbox	Rear Axle	Brakes	Fuel Tank Position	Vehicles to which applicable	Dates	Related Body Code	Description	Notes
1LT	16ft 6in	26ft 10⅜in	A145	D124	6¾ SF	3S	ON	LT1	1934-	LT1	54-seat outside stair	b.10185
1/2LT	16ft 6in	26ft 10⅜in	A145	D124	6¾ SF	3S	ON	LT2-150	1934-	LT2	60-seat outside stair square cab	
										LT2/1	do. round cab	LT21 to 2/2 LT 6/35
2/2LT	16ft 6in	26ft 10⅜in	A171	D124	6¾ SF	3S	ON	LT21	6/35-3/40	LT2/2		to 2/12LT3/4, 3/40
2LT	16ft 6in	26ft 8¼in	A145	D124	6¾ SF	3S	ON	LT151-950 with exceptions mentioned below	1934-40	LT3	56-seat inside stair	
										LT4	do. with tumblehome	169 to 12LT, 1933-4
										LT5	do. d-box in cab canopy	24 to 12LT, 1937
										LT5/1	do. 3 front, 2 rear d-boxes	rem to 1/12LT, 1939-40
3LT	16ft 6in	26ft 8¼in	A145	D128	6¾ SF	3S	ON	LT571, 588, 591, 592 and 20 others*	1934-	LT3/-2	As LT3 with midships f-trap	Originally LT549-552, 566-571
										LT5/2	As LT5 with midships f-trap	583-592
4LT	16ft 6in	27ft 0¾in	A161	D124	6¾ SF	3S	ON	LT191-9, 590, 643, 750-768, 948, 949	1934-	LT3	As LT3 with mods to suit o/e	Original bodies of LT 191-9
										LT5/3	with mods to suit o/e	
										LT5/4	LT5/1 with mods to suit o/e	
5LT	16ft 6in	26ft 11⅛in	A145	D124	6¾ SF	3S	ON	LT951-63/5-99, 1204-34/9-1329	1934	LT6	60-seat Bluebird type	to 11LT, 10/33-10/34
6LT	16ft 6in	26ft 11⅛in	A145	D124	6¾ SF	SH	ON	LT964, 1235-8, 1330-54	1934-	LT6/1	do. with midships fl-trap	
7LT	16ft 6in	27ft 3⅝in	A165	D124	5¾ SF	3S	ON	LT1375-1404	1934-	LT6/2	do. with mods to suit oil eng	to DI (A180) 1940-43
8LT	16ft 6in	27ft 3⅝in	A165	D128	5¾ SF	SH	ON	LT1355-74	1934-	LT6/3	do. with midships fl-trap	
9LT	16ft 6in	27ft 5in	6LW	D124	5¾ SF	3S	ON	LT741, 1417-26	1934-	LT7	Shortened Bluebird type	to 1/7LT6/5, (A180) 1944 onwards
10LT	16ft 6in	27ft 3⅝in	A165	D124	5¾ SF	3S	OS	LT1405-1416	1934-	LT8	modified Bluebird type	to DI (A180) 1940-43
11LT	16ft 6in	27ft 3⅝in	A165	D124	5¾ SF	3S	ON	LT951-63, 1204-34/9-1329	1934-	LT6/4	conversion from 5LT6	to D1 (A180) 1940-43
12LT	16ft 6in	27ft 0¾in	A165	D124	5¾ SF	3S	ON	169 buses (1933-4), 24 (1937)	1934-	LT3/1	from 2LT3	to DI(A180) 1940-43
										LT5/5	from 2LT5/1	
										LT5/6	from 2LT5	
1/12LT	16ft 6in	27ft 0¾in	A180	D124	5¾ SF	3S	ON	550 buses	1939-	LT3/3	from 2LT3	Included LT316 (ex-2LT4)
										LT5/7	from 2LT5/1	
										LT5/8	from 2LT5	
2/12LT	16ft 6in	26ft 8¼in	A171	D124	6¾ SF	3S	ON	LT21	3/40-	LT3/4	LT3 type modified	recoded with inside-stair body
1LTL	18ft 7in	29ft 5in	A140	D124	6¾ SF	3S	ON	LT1001-50, 1052-1136, 1138-1201	1934-	LTL1	35-seat sd with front d-box only	square-backed seats
										LTL1/1	35-seat sd with f and r d-boxes	round-backed seats
1/1LTL	18ft 7in	27ft 6in†	A145	D124	6¾ SF	3S	ON	LT1137	1935	LTL2	54-seat front entrance dd	ex-experimental coach
2LTL	18ft 7in	29ft 5in	A140	D124	6¾ SF	3S	ON	LT1427/8	1935	LTL3	As LTL1/1 excluding seats	Bluebird-type seats
3LTL	18ft 7in	30ft 0in	A140	D124	6¾ SF	3S	OS(2)	LT1429	1935	LTL4	Harrington 32 seat coach	

*from 1940 onwards LT271, 401/51/69/70, 571/3/80/2/8/91-3, 649/51/2/8/9 /62, 786/98, 827, 909/14, of which LT470, 592, 658, 909 were 3LT3/2, rest 3LT5/2   †approximate

Appendix 6: STL type Chassis codes, specifications and related body codes

Code	Wheelbase	Overall Length	Engine	Gearbox	Rear Axle	Brakes	Fuel Tank	Bonnet Numbers	Dates	Related Body Code	Description	Notes
1STL	16ft 3in	26ft 0in	A140	D124	6¼ SF†	SH	OS	STL1-49	1934-	STL1	LGOC 60-seat type	
2STL	16ft 3in	26ft 0in	A140	D124	6¼ FF	SH	OS	STL153-202	1934-	STL1	LGOC 60-seat type	
3STL	16ft 3in	26ft 0in	A140	D128	6¼ FF	SH	OS	STL50	1934-	STL1	LGOC 56-seat type	
3STL	16ft 3in	26ft 0in	A140	D128	6¼ FF	SH	OS	STL203-252	1934-9	STL2	LGOC 56-seat type	
4STL	16ft 3in	26ft 0in	A145	D128	5¾ FF	SH	OS	STL253-291	1934-9	STL3/2	First LPTB type	STL 253, 263, 290 to 1/4STL, 1938
1/4STL	16ft 3in	26ft 0in	A145	Sync	5¾ FF	SH	OS	STL253, 263, 290	1938-41	STL3/2	First LPTB type	
5STL	16ft 3in	26ft 0in	A171	D128*	5¾ FF	SH	OS	STL342-352	1934-	STL3/1	First LPTB type	
6STL	16ft 3in	26ft 0in	A145	D124	5¾ FF	SH	OS	STL292-341, 353-402	1934-	STL3	First LPTB type	Plus STL253, 263, 290 1941-
7STL	16ft 3in	26ft 0in	A145	D132	5¾ FF	SH	OS	STL403-552, 559-608	1934-9	STL3	First LPTB type	
8STL	16ft 3in	26ft 0in	A140	D124	6¼ SF†	SH	OS	STL51-130	1934-	STL4	Tilling type	
9STL	16ft 3in	26ft 0in	A171	D132	5¾ FF	SH	OS	STL609-758	1934-	STL5	LPTB standard. Bluebird seats	
1/9STL	16ft 3in	26ft 0in	A171	D132	5¾ FF	SH	OS	STL759-958	1935-	STL5/2	LPTB tubular seats (15 bodies)	
2/9STL	16ft 3in	26ft 0in	A171	D132	5¾ FF	SH	OS	STL1060-1259	1935-	STL11	LPTB tubular double-panelled	
3/9STL	16ft 3in	26ft 0in	A171	D132	5¾ FF	SH	OS	STL1264-1463, 1514-1613	1936-	STL11/1	b.15781 ex-full-fronted	
4/9STL	16ft 3in	26ft 0in	A171	D132	5¾ FF	SH	OS	STL1614-2515 with exc'ns	1936-	STL12	100 bodies with steel floor structure	STL2513/4/5 originally had A182 engine
5/9STL	16ft 3in	26ft 0in	A173	D132	5¾ FF	SH	OS	STL1642/54/7/61/8/70	1937-	STL13	40 Blackwall Tunnel bodies	
										STL14	Standard roof-box type	
										STL14/1	Standard roof-box type	later bodies and 12 spares
										STL15	175 Park Royal bodies	
10STL	16ft 3in	26ft 0in	A171	D132	5¾ FF		OS	STL959-1043, 1056-1059	1935-	STL6	First Country Series (Chiswick)	Increased from 48 to 52 seats 1939
1/10STL	16ft 3in	26ft 0in	A171	D132	5¾ FF		OS	STL1464-1513	1936-	STL6/1	Second Country Series (Weymann)	
11STL	16ft 3in	26ft 0in	A165	D124	5¾ FF		OS	STL1044-1055	1935-	STL7	Godstone low bridge type (Weymann)	
12STL	16ft 3in	26ft 0in	A140	D124	6¼ SF	3S	OS	STL553-6	1934-	STL8	Park Royal with Chiswick top deck	
1/12STL	16ft 3in	26ft 0in	A140	D124	6¼ SF	SH	OS	STL557	1934-			
13STL	16ft 3in	26ft 0in	A140	D128	6¼ SF	3S	OS	STL558	1934-	STL9	Birch conversion outside staircase	
14STL	15ft 6½in	25ft 0in	A171	D132	5¾ FF	SH	NS	STL1260-3	1936-	STL10	Dodson (STL1262) ex-DST5 Chiswick (STL1260/1/3) ex DST1-3	STL1262 later converted to 3/9STL12
15STL	16ft 3in	26ft 0in	A173	D132**	5¾ FF	SH	OS	STL2516-2647	1939-	STL16	1939 type	
16STL	16ft 3in	26ft 0in	A173	D132**	5¾ FF	SH	OS	STL403-552, 559-608	1939-	STL17	12 wartime bodies only	
1/16STL	16ft 3in	26ft 0in	A173	D128**	5¾ FF	SH	OS	STL254-262, 264-289, 291	1939-	STL18	conversion of STL3/2	
2/16STL	16ft 3in	26ft 0in	A173	D132**	5¾ FF	SH	OS	STL203-252	1939-	STL18/1	conversion of STL2	

†FF in some cases   *with internal dynamo drive   **with V-belt dynamo drive

Appendix 7: Q, C, STD, LTC, TF, CR and RT types. Chassis codes, specifications and corresponding body codes

Chassis Code	Wheelbase	Overall Length	Engine	Gearbox	Rear Axle	Brakes	Fuel Tank Position	Vehicles to which applicable	Dates	Related Body Code	Description	Notes
1Q	18ft 6in	27ft 6in	A167	4-sp	5.2 FF	3S	NS	Q1	1934-	Q1	Original Chiswick 37-seat sd	
2Q	15ft 10in	26ft 0in	A167	D129	6.2 FF	SH	NS	Q2, 3	1934-	Q2	MCCW front-entrance dd	
3Q	15ft 10in	26ft 0in	A167	D133	6.2 FF	SH	NS	Q4, 5	1935-	Q3	Weymann centre-entrance dd with doors	
4Q	18ft 6in	27ft 0in	A170	D133	5.2 FF	SH	NS	Q6-80	1935-	Q4	BRCW 35-seat centre-entrance sd	
1/4Q	18ft 6in	27ft 0in	A170	D133	5.2 FF	SH	NS	Q81-105, 186, 187	1935-	Q4/1	do. Coach version with heater etc	
5Q	16ft 6in	27ft 0in	A170	D133	5.2 FF	SH	NS	Q106-185	1936-	Q5	Park Royal 37-seat front-entrance sd	
6Q	18ft 6in	27ft 0in	A170	D133	5.2 FF	SH	NS	Q189-238	1937-	Q6	Park Royal 32-seat coach	
7Q	16ft 6in	27ft 0in	A170	D133	6.2 FF	Air	NS	Q188	1937-	Q7	Park Royal 51-seat dd coach	3-axle (model 0763)
1C	15ft 6in	24ft 0in	CP	4-sp	5.5 FF	SH	OS	C1	1934-	C1	Chiswick body	Exchanged with C51, 11/35
1/1C	15ft 6in	24ft 0in	CP	4-sp	5.5 FF	SH	NS	C76	1935-	C1/1	ex-St Albans & District	
2C	15ft 6in	24ft 0in	CO	4sp	5.5 FF	SH	OS	C2-75	1935-	C2	Short Bros all-metal Country Area	C51 to 1/2C and Central Area 11/35
1/2C	15ft 6in	24ft 0in	ZO	4-sp	5.5 FF	SH	NS	C77-98	1936-	C2/1	Weymann all-metal Central Area	
3C	15ft 6in	24ft 0in	ZP	4-sp	5.5 FF	SH	NS	C106-113	1936-	C3	Park Royal Inter-Station coaches	
1STD	16ft 3in	26ft 0in	O-8.6	4-sp	5.4 FF	SH	OS	STD1-90	1937-	STD1	Leyland all-metal	
2STD	16ft 3in	26ft 0in	O-8.6	TC	5.4 FF	SH	OS	STD91-100	1937-9	STD1		Converted to 1STD, 7-12/39
1LTC	16ft 6in	27ft 3in	A145	D132	6.8 FF	SH	OS	LTC1-24	1937-	LTC1	Weymann 30-seat sliding roof	
1TF	18ft 6in	27ft 6in	O-8.6	D132	5.4 FF	Air	NS	TF1	1937-	TF1	Leyland 34-seat b.18075	
2TF	18ft 6in	27ft 6in	O-8.6	D132	5.4 FF	Air	NS	TF14-88	1939-	TF2	Chiswick 34-seat Green Line	
								TF2-13	1939-	TF3	Park Royal 33-seat sightseeing	
1CR	15ft 6in	24ft 0in	CO	4-sp	5.5dD	SH	OS	CR1	1938-	CR1	b.18001	Country Area
2CR	15ft 6in	24ft 0in	ZO	4-sp	5.5dD	SH	OS	CR2-49	1939-	CR2	bb.224-271	CR12-16 originally green
1RT	16ft 4in	26ft 0in	A185	D140	5.17 FF	Air	NS	RT1	1939-	RT1	b.18246 Chiswick all-metal	
2RT	16ft 4in	26ft 0in	A185	D140	5.17 FF	Air	NS	RT2	1939-	RT2	bb.280-429. Chiswick composite	later 1/2RT2/1 (recip-compressor) and 3/2RT2/2